THE WILSON W. CLARK
MEMORIAL LIBRARY
UNIVERSITY OF PORTLAND

HEGEL ON SELF-CONSCIOUSNESS

PRINCETON MONOGRAPHS IN PHILOSOPHY

Harry G. Frankfurt, Series Editor

—————————————— ·ꟿꟿ· ——————————————

The Princeton Monographs in Philosophy series offers short historical and systematic studies on a wide variety of philosophical topics.

HEGEL ON SELF-CONSCIOUSNESS
Desire and Death in the
Phenomenology of Spirit

Robert B. Pippin

PRINCETON UNIVERSITY PRESS

PRINCETON AND OXFORD

B
2929
·P57
2011

·١ 13286298   #587249144

Copyright © 2011 by Princeton University Press

Published by Princeton University Press,
41 William Street, Princeton, New Jersey 08540

In the United Kingdom: Princeton University Press,
6 Oxford Street, Woodstock, Oxfordshire OX20 1TW

All Rights Reserved

ISBN 978-0-691-14851-9

Library of Congress Control Number: 2010935118

British Library Cataloging-in-Publication Data is available

This book has been composed in Janson

Printed on acid-free paper. ∞

press.princeton.edu

Printed in the United States of America

1 3 5 7 9 10 8 6 4 2

Contents

Acknowledgments

THE FOLLOWING is an expanded and revised version of the Spinoza Lectures given at the University of Amsterdam in April and May of 2009. The idea was to combine an interpretation of what I and many others regard as the most important chapter in all of Hegel—the fourth chapter of the *Phenomenology of Spirit*—with an essay about the philosophical significance of Hegel's ideas.

I am most grateful to the philosophy department at the University of Amsterdam for the opportunity to present these lectures and especially for the opportunity to live and teach in one of the world's most cultivated, interesting, and beautiful cities. For many small and large favors during my stay, I am especially indebted to the chair of the department Josef Früchtl, to my friend Beate Rössler, to Yolanda Verbeek for her kind and efficient attention to so many of the details of our visit, and to Marijke de Wit for her help with the administration of the masters seminar that I taught on Hegel's phenomenology of self-consciousness.

I began to discuss this interpretation of Hegel's theory of self-consciousness at a special symposium hosted by Colgate University in November 2008 (the Kokonas Symposium) and I am grateful to the philosophy department there for the invitation and for the many lively and illuminating discussions with members of the department and with students, and to my co-symposiasts, John McDowell and Robert Brandom, for their reaction and comments there and for their work in general, which I have always found inspiring. John McDowell's comments and correspondence after the event were especially beneficial in helping me clarify his (and my) understanding of this sometimes baffling, often profound, and clearly pivotal chapter in Hegel's work.

HEGEL ON SELF-CONSCIOUSNESS

·❡MP·

Introductory Remarks

ONE OF HEGEL'S MAIN concerns in the revolutionary book he wrote in the German city of Jena while only in his thirties, his *Phenomenology of Spirit*, is a familiar modern philosophical concern: the attempt to understand the various competencies involved in distinctly human sentience, sapience, and agency, and, especially and above all in Hegel's project, the complex inter-relations among all such competencies. So there are in his unprecedented book accounts of sensory receptivity, perception, judgment, generalization, inference, self-consciousness, nomic necessity, justification, as well as of intention, purpose, practical reason, linguistic community, and sociality in general. Hegel's account is unusual in that it is conducted via a procedure he invented, a "phenomenology," or what he at first called a "science of the experience of consciousness." This new procedure, at the very minimum and somewhat crudely summarized, involved imagining possible models of experience (models of its basic structure), primarily experience of objects and of other subjects, restricted to one or some set of competencies, or in some specific relation, and then demonstrating by a series of essentially *reductio ad absurdum* arguments that such an imagined experience, when imagined from the point of view of the experiencer, really could *not* be a possible or coherent experience, thus requiring some determinate addition or alteration to repair the imagined picture, and so a new possibility to be entertained. Eventually such an internal testing of models of experience becomes in the course of Hegel's developmental account so detailed and rich that it amounts to an examination of the possibility and viability of an actual historical form of life, a historical experience conducted under the assumption of such competencies and their inter-relationship. So once he has assembled all the materials necessary for a full, adequate picture of such a subject of experience (after the first five chapters), he then begins an even more unusual account of the development of such a subject, now a form of *collective* like-mindedness he calls *Geist*. From this point on, the account is even more unusual because Hegel treats the project of human self-knowledge as essentially a matter of what he calls *Geist*'s "actuality," its historical and social development, and he seems to effect a shift in the proper subject matter of philosophy itself, insisting that philosophy must not study mere concepts, but concepts *in* their "actuality," and that means in the *Phenomenology* in their historical actuality, when that actuality is considered in terms of this experiential "test."

So far, much of this should sound unusual but, aside from Hegel's highly idiosyncratic innovations in philosophical German, comprehensible and relatively trackable in the text. But there are two points in the progression of topics where puzzlement can easily become complete bafflement. They occur in the fourth chapter on "self-consciousness," a passage Hegel himself points to as the most important in the book, its "turning point." The first occurs when he suddenly claims: "Self-consciousness is desire itself (*Begierde überhaupt*)." The second is just as, if not more important, for Hegel's theory of self-consciousness and for post-Hegelian thought, and it is just as difficult to understand: the claim that "self-consciousness attains its satisfaction only in an-other self-consciousness."

I want to try to understand the meaning and philosophical motivation for these two claims in Hegel's adventurous book. Several qualifications are necessary, though, before embarking on such an enterprise. I will mention only the most serious, namely, that strictly speaking Hegel cannot be said to have a "theory" of self-consciousness in the usual sense, or at least that isolating such a theory does some violence to his famous holism. The entire *Phenomenology of Spirit* is a meditation on self-consciousness and the coming to self-consciousness of human subjects, especially as a kind of collective subject coming to collective self-consciousness, and Hegel treats as integral to this account everything from medieval Catholicism to the French Revolution. But as I hope to show in the following, the most distinctive, original aspect of that long account begins to come into focus in Chapter Four and that is sufficient reason for concentrating on that section alone.

There is another, broader reason for doing so, one more specific to the British and American tradition of philosophy. For several reasons philosophers like Aristotle, Descartes, and Kant continue to have a living presence in contemporary Anglophone philosophy (at least to some degree), and, by contrast, what is rather clumsily characterized as "European philosophy" has very little presence at the elite research universities.[1] One can make a good case that this supposedly divergent tradition began with Hegel and his influence on later European philosophy. There are two aspects to this influence. One has to do with the reluctance of those who philosophize under the shadow of Hegel to accept any firm separation between strictly epistemological or metaphysical

---

[1] "Clumsily" because much of what is characterized as analytic philosophy originated in Austrian and German philosophy.

issues or even broadly formal issues from various issues in what is traditionally considered practical philosophy, accounts of action, agency, purposiveness, interpretation, and the like. Such a holistic approach leads quickly to the second point of divergence, one that builds upon the integration of practical and theoretical philosophy: the post-Hegelian insistence on the relevance of human sociality and the historicity of that sociality in accounting for claims of cognitive success or even in understanding properly the nature of the basic mind-world and subject-subject relation inevitably presupposed in any account of the very possibility of epistemic or practical success. There are many forms of such claims for the philosophical relevance of such sociohistorical actuality to what had traditionally been considered strictly philosophical issues in epistemology, metaphysics, moral theory, aesthetics and so forth: socioeconomic matters in Marxism, genealogy and psychology in Nietzsche, mood and resoluteness in Heidegger and existentialism, archeology and genealogy in Foucault, the dependence of subject on structure (or the disappearance of subject into structure) in structuralism, and so forth. (The countercharge by more traditional philosophy has always been, of course, that such enterprises transform philosophy into something else, and so massively transform philosophy as to lose touch with it altogether.)

What I am calling the divergence between the traditions could plausibly be said to have originated in the turning point of this individual chapter in the *Phenomenology*—another reason for attending to it closely, even if in some violation of Hegel's holism. The book's turning point in other words involved a much broader turning point in the modern Western philosophical tradition, and so is especially valuable in the way it can highlight the issue: transformation of philosophy, or a farewell to philosophy altogether?

And a strategy naturally suggests itself at this point. Since the topic of the chapter, self-consciousness, together with another to which it is deeply linked, freedom, are far and away the most important topics in what we call German Idealism, I propose to begin with the introduction of the idea of the centrality of self-consciousness in human sapience by Immanuel Kant. For that is the position, I want to show, that Hegel is building on and transforming in the direction just suggested.[2]

---

[2] The following represents a reconsideration and substantial alteration of the interpretation of Chapter Four I originally presented in *Hegel's Idealism: The Satisfactions of Self-Consciousness* (Cambridge: Cambridge University Press, 1989) (hereafter HI). If anything, I am more committed here to what Scott Jenkins, in "Hegel's Concept of Desire," *Journal of the History of Philosophy* 47, no. 1 (2009), pp. 109–30, calls a "contextualist" approach; that is, working within the limitations of what has been developed in the first three chapters in order to explain why there seem to be so many new topics, rather than just helping oneself to "an appeal to the capacities of rational, sentient beings" in general (109) as Jenkins does. I think the present account answers some of the concerns raised by Jenkins (110–12). In general, Jenkins wants to press the point that Hegel should not be seen here as primarily concerned with a further elaboration of the conditions of knowing (which he sees me doing in HI), but rather as advancing a broad, powerful claim about the nature of human subjectivity as such, that that is his *new* theme. He goes on to deny that this subjectivity should be understood as a mere "point of view," insisting instead that it is a corporeal, historical, laboring subject. It seems to me truer to the radicality of Hegel's attempt to admit that he is indeed on about such themes, but in the service of a further elaboration of the possibility of intentional consciousness. Put another way, Jenkins does not seem to me to do justice (as McDowell does in an interpretation we shall look at shortly) to Hegel's formulation in ¶167 that *in* self-consciousness, "the whole breadth of the sensuous world is preserved for it." It is true that there is a great deal to say about the content of a self-relation in relation to an object before the properly epistemological focus returns, but Hegel never loses sight of it. See also my concluding remarks about "wholeness."

Chapter One

On Hegel's Claim That Self-Consciousness Is "Desire Itself" (Begierde überhaupt)

I

KANT HELD THAT what distinguishes an object in our experience from the mere subjective play of representations is rule-governed unity. His famous definition of an object is just "that in the concept of which a manifold is united" (B137). This means that consciousness itself must be understood as a discriminating, unifying activity, paradigmatically as judging, and not as the passive recorder of sensory impressions. Such a claim opens up a vast territory of possibilities and questions since Kant does not mean that our awake attentiveness is to be understood as something we *intentionally do*, in the standard sense, even if it is not also a mere event that happens to us, as if we happen to be triggered into a determinate mental state, or as if sensory stimuli just activate an active mental machinery.

Kant also clearly does not mean to suggest by his claim that the form of consciousness is a judgmental form that consciousness consists of thousands of very rapid judgmental claims being deliberately made, thousands of "S is P's" or "If A then B's" taking place. The world is taken to be such and such without such takings being isolatable, intentional judgments. What Kant *does* mean by understanding consciousness as "synthetic" is quite a formidable, independent topic in itself.[1]

Kant's main interest in the argument of the deduction was to show first that the rules governing such activities (whatever the right way to describe such activities) cannot be wholly empirical rules, all derived from experience, that there must be rules for the derivation of such rules that cannot themselves be derived, or that there must be pure concepts of the understanding; and second, that these non-derived rules have genuine "objective validity," are not mere subjective impositions on an independently received manifold, that, as he puts it, the a priori prescribed "synthetic unity of consciousness" "is not merely a condition that I myself require in knowing an object, but is a condition under which any intuition must stand in order to become an object for me" (B138). Kant seems to realize that he gives the impression that for him consciousness is a two-step process—the mere reception of sensory data, and then the conceptualization of such data—but he works hard in the pursuit of the second desideratum to disabuse his readers of that impression.

Aside from some Kant scholars, there are not many philosophers who still believe that Kant proved in this argument that we possess synthetic a priori knowledge, although there is wide admiration for the power of Kant's arguments about, at least, causality and substance. But there remains a great deal of interest in his basic picture of the nature of

---

[1] I present an interpretation of the point in "What Is Conceptual Activity?" forthcoming in *The Myth of the Mental?* ed. J. Shear.

conscious mindedness. For the central component of his account, judgment, is, as already noted, not a mental event that
merely happens, as if causally triggered into its synthetic activity by sensory stimuli. Judging, while not a practical action initiated by a decision, is nevertheless an *activity* sustained and resolved, sometimes in conditions of uncertainty,
by a subject and that means that it is normatively structured.
The categorical rules of judgment governing such activity
are rules about what ought to be judged, how our experience
ought to be (must be) organized. For example, we distinguish
or judge successive perceptions of a stable object as really
simultaneous in time, and not actually representing something successive. This is a distinction that we must make; we
experience successiveness in both cases and must be able to
determine what ought to be judged simultaneous and what
actually successive.[2] So such rules are not rules describing
how we do operate, are not psychological laws of thought,
but involve a responsiveness to normative proprieties. And,
to come to the point of contact with Hegel that is the subject
of the following, this all means that consciousness must be
inherently *reflective* or *apperceptive*. (I cannot be *sustaining an
activity*, implicitly trying to get, say, the objective temporal
order right in making up my mind, without in some sense
knowing I am so taking the world to be such, or without

---

[2] To be as clear as possible: we do not have an option or choice about
the necessary distinguishability in our experience between accidental succession and causal succession. Experience would not be possible were
there not this distinguishability, Kant argues in the Second Analogy. But
that necessity is conceptual, not psychological (no concept of experience would be intelligible without the distinction and it being possible in
principle for experiencers to make it), and we *do* actually have to determine *which* successions are accidental and which causally necessary, and
that requires the activity of judgmental discrimination. We can thus get
this wrong.

apperceptively taking it so. I am taking or construing rather than merely recording because I am also in such taking holding open the possibility that I may be taking falsely.) So all consciousness is inherently, though rarely explicitly, self-conscious. It is incorrect to think of a conscious state as just filled with the rich details of a house-perception, as if consciousness merely registers its presence; I take or judge the presence of a house, not a barn or gas station; or in Kant's famous formula: "the '*I think*' must be able to accompany all my representations." But what could be meant by "inherently," or "*in some sense* knowing I am taking or judging it to be such and such"? In *what* sense am I in *a relation to myself* in any conscious relation to an object? That is, the claim is that all consciousness involves a kind of self-consciousness, taking S to be P and thus taking myself to be taking S to be P. But in a self-relation like this, the self in question cannot be just another object of intentional awareness. If it were, then there would obviously be a regress problem. By parity of whatever reasoning established that the self must be able to *observe* itself as an object in taking anything to be anything, one would have to also argue that the *observing* self must also be observable, and so on. The self-relation, whatever it is, cannot be a two-place intentional relation, and the self-consciousness of consciousness cannot invite a two-stage or two-element picture: our conscious sentience and then, in addition, our self-monitoring self-relation. (As Kant and Hegel would put it: the latter is just consciousness again and we have not found self-consciousness.)[3]

---

[3] The post-Kantian philosopher who first made a great deal out of this point was Fichte, and the modern commentator who has done the most to work out the philosophical implications of the point has been Dieter Henrich, starting with *Fichtes ursprüngliche Einsicht* (Frankfurt: Klostermann, 1967).

Hegel's own most famous discussion of these issues is found in the first four chapters of his 1807 *Phenomenology of Spirit* (hereafter PhG).The first three chapters of that book are grouped together under the heading "Consciousness" and the fourth chapter is called simply "Self-Consciousness." (That fourth chapter has only one subsection, called "The Truth of Self-Certainty," and that will be the focus of the following discussion.)[4] Accordingly, especially given the extraordinarily sweeping claims Hegel makes about his indebtedness to the Kantian doctrine of apperception,[5] one would expect that these sections have something to do with the Kantian points noted earlier, and so with the issue of the self-conscious character of experience and the conditions for the possibility of experience so understood. But there has been a lot of understandable controversy about the relation between the first three chapters of the PhG and the fourth. Since the fourth chapter discusses desire, life, a

[4] This is quite a typical Hegelian title, and can be misleading. By "The Truth of Self-Certainty" (*Die Wahrheit der Gewißheit seiner selbst*), Hegel does *not* mean, as he seems to, the truth *about* the self's actual certainty of itself. He actually means, as we shall see, that the truth of self-certainty is not a matter of self-certainty at all, just as sense-certainty was not in the end certain. This relation between subjective certainty and its "realization in truth" is the key to the basic structure of the PhG. Its most elementary form is something like: the truth of the "inner" (any putative self-certainty) is the "outer" (a mediated relation to the world and to others), all in distinction from anything that might be suggested by the title (as in: how to explain the *fact* of such self-certainty). I am disagreeing here with Jenkins in the article cited earlier, p. 114.

[5] "It is one of the profoundest and truest insights to be found in the *Critique of Pure Reason* that the unity which constitutes the unity of the *Begriff* is recognized as the original synthetic unity of apperception, as the unity of the I think, or of self-consciousness." *Wissenschaft der Logik*, Bd. 12 in *Gesammelte Werke*, ed. Rheinisch-Westfälischen Akademie der Wissenschaften (Hamburg: Felix Meiner, 1968–), p. 221; *Science of Logic*, trans. A.V. Miller (Amherst: Humanity Books, 1969), p. 584.

struggle to the death for recognition between opposed subjects, and a resulting Lord-Bondsman social structure, it has
not been easy to see how the discussion of sense-certainty,
perception, and the understanding is being *continued*. Some
very influential commentators, like Alexandre Kojève, pay
almost no attention to the first three chapters. They write
as if we should isolate the Self-Consciousness chapter as a
free-standing philosophical anthropology, a theory of the
inherently violent and class-riven nature of human sociality.
(There are never simply human beings as such in Kojève's
account. Our species status as one and all equal free subjects
must be collectively achieved, and until the final bloody revolution ushers in a classless society, there are only Masters
and Slaves.) Others argue that in Chapter Four, Hegel simply changes the subject to the problem of sociality. We can
see why it might be natural for him to change the subject at
this point, for it is a different subject. (Having introduced the
necessary role of self-consciousness in consciousness, Hegel
understandably changes the topic to very broad and different and independent questions like: what, in general, *is* self-
consciousness? What is a self? What is it to be a being "for
which" things can be, to use Brandom's language, who offers
his own version of the change-of-subject interpretation?)[6]

---

[6] There are other interpretations which tend to isolate the argument
in Chapter Four in other ways, construing it as a kind of "transcendental
argument" that aims to prove that the "consciousness of one's self requires
the recognition of another self." Axel Honneth, "Von der Begierde zur
Anerkennung: Hegels Begründung von Selbstbewußtsein," in *Hegels Phä-
nomenologie des Geistes: Ein kooperativer Kommentar zu einem Schlüsselwerk
der Moderne*, ed. K. Vieweg and W. Welsch (Frankfurt a.M.: Suhrkamp,
2008). On that issue itself (*"from* desire *to* recognition") and on the one
and a half pages of argument in Hegel that seek to establish this, Honneth
has a number of valuable things to say. But, as I will be arguing, no con-
vincing interpretation of the chapter is possible that does not explain the

More recently, some commentators, like John McDowell and Pirmin Stekeler-Weithofer, have argued that there is actually neither a new beginning nor a shift in topics in Chapter Four. In McDowell's treatment the problem is an extension and development of the one that emerged in the first three chapters but still basically concerns that issue: how to understand the right "equipoise" between independence and dependence in the relations between subjects and objects. What appear to be the orectic[7] and social issues of Chapter Four are for McDowell "figures" or analogies for what remains the problem of the mind's passive dependence on objects and active independence of them in our experience of the world, in just the sense sketched previously in the summary of Kant (i.e., neither independent subjective imposition, nor merely passive receptive dependence). What we have is a picture of our active, spontaneous self in a kind of mythic confrontation and struggle *with its own* passive empirical self, struggling at first futilely, for radical independence, and then an initial but doomed relation of

---

underlying structure of the "*Consciousness*-Self-Consciousness" argument in the book as a whole. And I don't believe that Honneth's very brief remarks about understanding ourselves as "creators of true claims" or "the rational individual . . . aware of its constitutive, world-creating [*welterzeugenden*] cognitive acts" (p. 190) presents that structure accurately. "World-creating" is much too abstract and so imprecise a term to capture what Hegel is trying to say about intentional consciousness and its implications for his phenomenology.

[7] I use this Aristotelian term in distinction from Brandom's term for the connative dimensions of consciousness, "erotic," because the latter seems a bit misleading, contains the vague though delightful suggestion that all consciousness has a sexual dimension, and because Hegel's account seems to me suffused with an Aristotelian spirit. See Aristotle's discussion in Book VI of the *Nichomachean Ethics* on choice (*proairesis*) as either "desiring intellect" [*orektikos nous*] or "minded desire" [*orexis dianoêtikê*], 1139b5–6.

dominance (as if the soul tries to make of its own corporeal nature a *Knecht* or mere servant).[8] So for McDowell, Hegel does not mean to introduce in a direct sense the topic of desire as a necessary element in the understanding of *consciousness* itself (as the text, however counterintuitively, would seem to imply). Rather, says McDowell, "'Desire überhaupt' functions as a figure for the general idea of 'negating otherness' (admittedly an orectic issue of some sort), by appropriating or consuming, incorporating into oneself what at first figures as merely other, something that happens in perception, say."[9] And "life," the next topic in the chapter, is said to exemplify the structure of *der Begriff*; let us say: the basic logical structure of all possible intelligibility, all sense-making.[10] The struggle to the death for recognition is said to be a rich and colorful "allegory" of the possible relations of

[8] Not that McDowell wants to say that this picture of dual and opposed elements remains Hegel's picture, with at some point just a kind of compromise or peace treaty. The *whole* picture of such a duality between apperceptive and passive-sensible elements or stages is what must be given up in McDowell's picture too. I want to say that giving this up is part and parcel of giving up a picture of opposed self-consciousnesses who ultimately reach some sort of compromise. Hegel's picture is much more radical and his argument for it begins here, in this chapter.

[9] John McDowell, "The Apperceptive I and the Empirical Self: Towards a Heterodox Reading of 'Lordship and Bondage' in Hegel's *Phenomenology*" (hereafter AI) in *Hegel: New Directions*, ed. Katerina Deligiorgi (Chesham: Acumen, 2007), p. 38.

[10] Especially the relation between universal and particular, as is clearest in ¶169. And there is a good deal of truth in that characterization. The experiencing subject inevitably becomes aware of itself as a living being *of a kind*, a species form it shares with all other such beings, all sharing the generic form of life, and itself as a *singular* subject, whose own life is not "life" in general or its species life. (Thus, McDowell would point out, his interpretation is not overly or excessively allegorical. It is important to his account, he says (in correspondence), that life be *life*, not a figure for something other than life.)

both independent and dependent sides *within one conscious-ness*. And so McDowell asserts that Chapter Four does not yet directly introduce the issue of sociality at all, despite the famous phrase there about the new presence of an "I that is a We and a We that is an I."

This interpretation has the very great virtue of preserving a connection with the first three chapters, but, as I will argue, while the general issue of the logic of the relation between independence and dependence is certainly applicable to the relation between spontaneous apperception and the passive empirical self, McDowell's interpretation, however rich in itself, fails to do justice to the radicality of what Hegel actually proposes. I want to argue that when Hegel says that self-consciousness *is* "desire überhaupt"[11] he means that to be relevant to the question of the apperceptive nature of consciousness itself; and that *thereby* he provides the basis for the claim that self-consciousness attains its satisfaction only in another self-consciousness.[12] Defending that interpretation is the task of this book.

[11] Hegel's developmental procedure here requires a general cautionary note. The identification of self-consciousness with desire occurs at a very early stage, as Hegel begins to assemble the various dimensions and elements he thinks we will need in order to understand the self-conscious dimension of consciousness. Initially Hegel is only saying: we have *at least* to understand that self-consciousness must be understood as mere desire (another sensible translation of "*Begierde überhaupt*"). It will prove impossible to consider such self-consciousness as merely desire and *nothing else*, and that impossibility is the rest of the story of the chapter. But this procedure means that from now on self-consciousness must be still understood as inherently orectic, whatever else it is.

[12] Brandom also thinks of the PhG as an allegory, in his case an allegory of various dimensions of the issue of conceptual content. Robert Brandom, "The Structure of Desire and Recognition: Self-Consciousness and Self-Constitution," *Philosophy and Social Criticism*, 33 (2007) (hereafter SDR). For example, he thinks of Hegel's treatment of the struggle to the death as a "metonymy" for the issue of commitment (of "really" being

So here stated all at once is the thesis I would like to attribute to Hegel. (That is, the thesis worked out and defended in Chapter Four. As noted, the entire book is a meditation on self-consciousness, on the becoming self-consciousness of *Geist*.) I think that Hegel's position is that we misunderstand all dimensions of self-consciousness, from apperception in consciousness itself, to simple, explicit reflection about myself, to practical self-knowledge of my own so-called identity, by considering any form of it as in any way observational or inferential or immediate or any sort of two-place intentional relation. However we come to know anything about ourselves (or whatever self-relation is implicit in attending to the world), it is not by observing an object, nor by conceptualizing an inner intuition, nor by any immediate self-certainty or direct presence of the self to itself. From the minimal sense of being aware of being determinately conscious at all (of judging), to complex avowals of who I am, of my own identity and deep commitments, Hegel, I want to say, treats self-consciousness as (i) a practical *achievement* of some sort.[13] Such a relation must be understood as

---

committed). But it is only that, one of many possible exemplifications of what it means in fact to have the commitment that one avows. Being willing to lose one's job, for example, could be another exemplification. Here and throughout, I want to resist such allegorical or figurative interpretations in both Brandom's and McDowell's accounts. I discuss Brandom's interpretation in the next chapter. (Denying allegorical readings, one should note immediately, does not mean, by contrast, to imply a claim that Hegel is talking about something historical or literal. The chapter *is* a philosophical fable of sorts but its elements do not stand at some figurative remove from what they seem to be about, any more than Hobbes on the state of nature or Rousseau on the solitary savage are allegorical in that sense.)

[13] This is contrary to the interpretation by Fred Neuhouser, "Desire, Recognition, and the Relation between Bondsman and Lord," in *The Blackwell Guide to Hegel's Phenomenology*, ed. K. Westphal (Oxford: Wiley-Blackwell, 2009), pp. 37–54, who argues that Hegel in effect changes the

the *result of an attempt*, never, as it certainly seems to be, as an immediate presence of the self to itself, and it often requires some sort of striving, even struggle (and all of this even in accounting for the self-conscious dimension of ordinary perceptual experience). Self-consciousness, in all its forms, is some mode of mindedness that we must achieve (be continually achieving), and that must mean: can ultimately fail to achieve fully and once having achieved can lose. It is nothing like turning the mind's eye inward to inspect itself.[14]

---

subject from apperception to a practical self-conception and self-evaluation. I think Hegel's presentation is motivated by the internal inadequacies of the Kantian notion of apperception *in general*. Without that issue in view, we won't have a sense of *why* the problem of self-consciousness's unity with itself should emerge here, why such a unity "must become essential to it," and the discussion of a single self-conscious being certain of its own radical and complete independence (*Selbstständigkeit*) will have to appear unmotivated, simply a new theme. Cf. p. 42.

[14] This is a potentially quite misleading way of putting the point, but I can't think of a better way. As baldly stated, it seems to imply that some "failed self-consciousness" could be imagined wandering around, unable to have determinate experience of objects, perhaps in the "less than a dream" state once entertained by Kant. Qualifications galore on the "achievement" notion will begin presently, but it must be stressed that this achievement language refers primarily to collective mutually recognitive mindedness, is not a matter of individual achievement or one which invites any real historical genealogy, and that, however initially counterintuitive, there *is* some sense in which Hegel *does* want to maintain that under some forms of normative self-regulation—so deeply habitual, shared, and taken for granted as to be almost inaccessible to reflection—some community can be said to prevent, to deny itself, a proper responsiveness to defeasibility and challenge constitutive of what will turn out to be proper or successful (non-distorted) experience. Hegel's point is not that archaic subjects who responded to natural forces as purposive agents held false beliefs ultimately corrected by empirical disconfirmation. Although the beliefs *were* false, his point is that they held each other to account and experienced the world in ways not open to such disconfirmation. So the account of the collapse of such a practice must look elsewhere for the proper explanation, to *Geist*'s "experience of itself." This

Admittedly, it seems *very* hard to understand why anyone would think that my awareness, say, not just of the contents of a lecture I am giving, but whatever kind of awareness I have of my being in the process of giving a lecture, of actually following appropriate lecturing rules, should involve any such practical activity or achievement. It seems effortless to be so self-aware; there is no *felt* desire or striving or struggle involved, and as a report of what seems to me to be the case, it even appears incorrigible. But Hegel wants to claim that as soon as we properly see the error of holding that the self in any self-awareness is immediately present to an inspecting mind, or that it is a higher level mode of self-monitoring, his own interpretation is just thereby implied. If the self's relation to itself *cannot* be immediate or direct or "of an object," but if some self-relation is a condition of intentional awareness, the conclusion that it is some sort of *to-be-achieved* follows for him straightforwardly.[15] Even a minimal form of self-conscious taking-to-be-so opens up the possibility of taking falsely or in a way inconsistent with other (or all) such takings and so sets a certain sort of task. More on this in a minute; this is the

---

"achievement" language accompanies almost all of Hegel's discussions of *Geist*, especially about the achieved status of freedom, a topic deeply connected to the self-consciousness issue. And as in other dimensions of this issue, the achievement is not something I *set out to do*. It is constitutively part of what it is to be open to the world as a human experiencer. See *Hegels Philosophie des subjektiven Geistes/Hegel's Philosophy of Subjective Spirit*, 3 volumes, ed. and trans. M. Petry (Dordrecht: Riedel, 1978), I, pp. 52–3 (hereafter PSS). I am indebted to Terry Pinkard for correspondence about this point.

[15] So self-consciousness, while not "thetic," to use the Sartrean word, or intentional or positional, is not sort of or vaguely positional, caught at the corner of our eye, or glimpsed on the horizon. It is not intentional or object-directed at all. Jean-Paul Sartre, *The Transcendence of the Ego: An Existentialist Theory of Consciousness* (New York: Hill and Wang, 1991).

central motive for *his* version of the claim that consciousness is apperceptive.[16]

Another way of putting this point, one that ties in with almost every aspect of Hegel's philosophical approach, would

[16] John McDowell has suggested (in a response to a presentation of an
earlier version of this lecture at the Kokonas Symposium at Colgate University in November 2008) that the notion of "achievement" is a misleading term here, that whatever achievement is involved in being able to
judge apperceptively should be understood along the model of learning
a language, of simply being initiated into a linguistic community, something that involves no notion of struggle or practical achievement in the
usual sense. It just happens. But (a) Hegel is here describing the minimal
conditions for such a capacity to be in effect and it is only as he explores
the implications of the realization of this capacity that he introduces the
orectic and social issues that follow; and (b) what Hegel is describing *is*
like the acquisition of a linguistic capacity as long as we admit that such
an acquisition finally has to involve much more than acquiring rules of
grammatical correctness. To be initiated into a linguistic community is to
be initiated into all the pragmatic dimensions of appropriateness, authority, who gets to say what, when, and why. One is not a competent speaker
as such until one has learned such matters of linguistic usage, and Hegel
wants to treat such norms in terms of their historical conditions, primarily
in this chapter the social conditions and social conflict "behind" any such
norms. See also McDowell's "On Pippin's Postscript," in *Having the World
in View* (Cambridge, Mass.: Harvard University Press, 2009), pp. 185–203
(hereafter HWV). Cf. Habermas's account of what a full pragmatics of
language has to take in, how full initiation into a linguistic community
means that speakers "no longer relate *straightaway* to something in the
objective, social, or subjective worlds; instead they relativize their utter-
ances against the possibility that their validity will be contested by other
actors." Jürgen Habermas, *The Theory of Communicative Action, Reason
and the Rationalization of Society*, vol. I (Boston: Beacon Press, 1984), pp.
98–99. In Hegel's account, the standards for this unique kind of challenge
to a speaker or agent cannot be made out transcendentally or "quasi-tran-
scendentally," as Habermas sometimes says, but will require the unusual
reconstructive phenomenology under consideration here. (For those who
know Habermas: this also means that there is not that strict distinction
possible, so important to Habermas, between the "logic of historical self-
education" in, and the transcendental "logic of justification" for, norms.
Insisting on such a distinction is why Habermas is not a Hegelian.)

be to note that if self-consciousness or any form of taking oneself to be or being committed to anything is not introspective or observational, then it must always be *provisional*. Such a self-regard requires some confirmation or realization out in the world and for others if it is to count as what it is taken to be. The clearest examples of this occur in Hegel's theory of agency where one cannot be said to actually have had the intention or commitment one avows, even sincerely avows, until one actually realizes that intention and the action turns out to count as that action in the social world within which it is enacted. (And of course, people can come to find out that their actual intentions, as manifested in what they actually are willing to do, can be very different from those they avow, even sincerely avow.)[17]

And (ii)[18] Hegel sees such an attempt and achievement as necessarily involving a relation to other people, as inherently social. This last issue about the role of actualization begins to introduce such a dependence, but it is hard to see at the outset why other people need be involved in the intimacy and privacy that seems to characterize my relation to myself.

His case for looking at things this way has three main parts. In a way that is typical of his procedure, he tries to begin with the most theoretically thin or simple form of the required self-relation and so first considers the mere sentiment of self that a living being has in *keeping itself alive*, where *keeping itself alive* reflects this minimal reflective *attentiveness to self*. Such a minimal form of self-relatedness is shown not to establish the sort of self-relatedness (normative self-determination) required as the desideratum in the

---

[17] This issue is the central one and is explored at length in my *Hegel's Practical Philosophy: Rational Agency as Ethical Life* (Cambridge: Cambridge University Press, 2008).

[18] (i) was the "practical achievement" claim.

first three chapters. He then asks what alters when the object of the desires relevant to maintaining life turns out not to be just another object or obstacle but another subject. In effect, he argues that everything changes when our desires are not just thwarted or impeded, but challenged and refused. And he then explores how the presence of such an other subject, in altering what could be a possible self-relation, sets a new agenda for the rest of the *Phenomenology*, for the problems of both sapience and agency.

II

The central passage where the putative "practical turn" in all this takes place is the following:

> But this opposition between its [self-consciousness's] ap-pearance and its truth has only the truth for its essence, namely, the unity of self-consciousness with itself. This unity must become essential to self-consciousness, which is to say, self-consciousness is *desire* itself. (¶167) ("*Be-gierde überhaupt*," which could also be translated as "desire in general," or "desire, generally" or "mere desire." I am following here Terry Pinkard's translation.)[19]

The passage presupposes the larger issue we have been setting out—the way Hegel has come to discuss the dou-ble nature of consciousness (consciousness of an object, a this-such, and the non-positional consciousness or implicit

---

[19] Pinkard's translation is a valuable facing-page translation and is available at http://web.mac.com/titpaul/Site/About_Me_files/Phenomenology%20of%20Spirit%20%28entire%20text%29.pdf

The paragraph numbers in the text refer to his translation as well.

awareness of my taking it to be this-such).[20] He discusses
this as what he calls an "opposition," or, as he says, the "negativity" that this doubleness introduces within consciousness, the fact that consciousness is not simply absorbed into
("identified with") its contents, but has also, let us say, taken
up a position toward what it thinks.[21] To understand this, we
need the following passage from the Introduction:

> However, consciousness is for itself its concept, and as
> a result it immediately goes beyond the restriction, and,
> since this restriction belongs to itself, it goes beyond itself
> too. (¶80)[22]

[20] As self-consciousness, consciousness henceforth has a doubled object:
the first, the immediate object, the object of sense-certainty and perception, which, however, is marked *for it* with the *character of the negative*; the
second, namely, *itself*, which is the true *essence* and which at the outset is
on hand merely in opposition to the first. (¶167)

[21] His formulation later in the *Berlin Phenomenology* is especially clear:

> There can be no consciousness without self-consciousness. I
> know something, and that about which I know something I
> have in the certainty of myself [*das wovon ich weiss habe ich in
> der Gewissheit meiner selbst*] otherwise I would know nothing
> of it; the object is my object, it is other and at the same time
> mine, and in this latter respect I am self-relating.

G.W.F. Hegel: The Berlin Phenomenology, trans. M. Petry (Dordrecht:
Riedel, 1981), p. 55 (hereafter BPhG).

[22] He also introduces here a claim that will recur much more promi-
nently in this account of the difference between animal and human desire:

> However, to knowledge, the goal is as necessarily fixed as the
> series of the progression. The goal lies at that point where
> knowledge no longer has the need to go beyond itself, that
> is, where knowledge works itself out, and where the concept
> corresponds to the object and the object to the concept.
> Progress towards this goal is thus also unrelenting, and sat-
> isfaction [n.b. the introduction of *Befriedigung*] is not to be
> found at any prior station on the way. What is limited to
> a natural life is not on its own capable of going beyond its

He is actually making two claims here. The first is the premise of his inference: that "consciousness is for itself its concept." The idea seems to be: If we understand this first premise properly, we will understand why he feels entitled to the "and as a result," the claim that consciousness is thereby immediately "beyond" any such restriction or concept that it sets "for itself." (I want to claim that this all amounts to a defense of the claim that consciousness must be understood as apperceptive.) He means to say that the normative standards and proprieties at play in human consciousness are "consciousness's own," that is, are *followed* by a subject, are not psychological, empirical laws of thought, to return to the point made earlier. This is his version of the Kantian principle that persons are subject to no law or norm other than ones they have subjected themselves to.[23] (This is what is packed into the "for itself" here.) This does not mean either in Kant or in Hegel that there are episodes of self-subjection or explicit acts of allegiance or anything as ridiculous as all that; just that norms governing what we think and do can be said to govern thought and action only insofar as subjects, however implicitly or habitually or unreflectively (or as a matter of "second-nature"), accept such constraints and sustain allegiance; they follow the rules, are not governed by them. It is only because of this that someone like Socrates or Galileo or Freud can occasion intellectual crises. (As all the post-Wittgensteinean discussion of rule-following has

---

immediate existence. However, it is driven out of itself by something other than itself, and this being torn out of itself is its death. (¶80)

[23] This principle is of course primarily at home in Kant's practical philosophy, but it is also at work in the theoretical philosophy, particularly where Kant wants to distinguish his own account of experiential mindedness from Locke's or Hume's.

shown, there cannot be any rules for the following of these rules, so one can be said to be following such rules in carrying out what is required without any explicit calculation of how to do so.) How the allegiance gets instituted and how it can lose its grip are matters Hegel is very interested in, but it has nothing to do with individuals "deciding" about allegiances at moments of time. Or, to invoke Kant again, knowers and doers are not explicable as beings subject to laws of nature (although as also ordinary objects, they *are* so subject), but by appeal to their representation of laws and self-subjection to them.[24]

And Hegel means this to apply in ordinary cases of perceptual knowledge too. I know what would count as good perceptual reasons for an empirical claim on the basis of whatever "shape of spirit" or possible model of experience is under consideration at whatever stage in the PhG. That is, Hegel considers empirical rules of discrimination, unification, essence/appearance distinctions, conceptions of explanation, etc., as normative principles, and he construes some set of these as a possible determinate whole, as all being

---

[24] So I think that Sebastian Rödl is wrong when he says that Kant's autonomy doctrine can have it that laws for action can be "one's own" by having a certain "logical form"; see *Self-Consciousness* (Cambridge, Mass.: Harvard University Press, 2007), p. 117. Kant's own famous account of autonomy states unambiguously that I must be able to regard myself as the "author" [*Urheber*] of the law. I. Kant, *Foundations of the Metaphysics of Morals*, trans. L.W. Beck (New York: Macmillan, 1990), p. 48. Rödl apparently thinks that any notion of "giving oneself the law" would involve "arbitrary, lawless" acts (ibid.). But this is not so; it is quite possible to interpret Kant's clear insistence on self-legislation without any bizarre moment of Sartrean election. The whole point of starting out by noting that Kant's formulation is paradoxical is to insist that, whatever he means by the "*Urheber*" language, he *cannot* mean *that*, arbitrary willing. See my *Hegel's Practical Philosophy*, and the critique therein of Korsgaard, Chapter Three.

simply manifestations of the overriding requirements of a "shape of spirit" considered in this idealized isolation of capacities that makes up Chapters One through Five, and he cites possible illustrations of such a shape and such internal contradictions (determinate illustrative actual cases like trying to say "this here now," or trying to distinguish the thing which bears properties from those properties). The concepts involved in organizing perceptual experience are also norms prescribing how the elements of perceptual experience ought to be organized (especially in Kant temporally organized) and so they do not function like fixed physiological dispositions. We are responsive to a perceivable environment in norm-attentive ways.

Another way to put this would be to say that our discriminated attentiveness never occurs episodically, but as part of a totality or whole within which any such discrimination must fit, and so any such attentiveness is subject to a certain sort of strain when it threatens not to fit. That totality is a norm, not a law of thought. On a certain (empiricist) way of thinking, it can seem very odd to say that such a totality and its proprieties can be in any sense held in mind, that one is attentive "in the light" of such a totality and its requirements, without that totality being another idea or representation one attends to. But that would be most paradoxical. Such an idea would just be another one in and subject to the requirements of such a totality, and we would be no better and much worse off postulating it. This issue is of a piece with the same deeply misleading temptation to think that any "achievement" language, like that introduced earlier, must refer to a separate enterprise I set out to accomplish after I realize something about a claim or practical project.

Finally—and this is the most important indication of their normative status—since the principles involved guide my behavior or conclusions only insofar as they are accepted and followed, they can prove themselves inadequate, and lose their grip. This is what Hegel means in the conclusion of his inference by saying that consciousness "immediately goes beyond this restriction." It is always "beyond" any norm in the sense that it is not, let us say, stuck with such a restriction as a matter of psychological fact; consciousness is always in a position to alter norms for correct perception, inferring, law-making, or right action. Perception of course involves physiological processes that are species-identical across centuries and cultures, but perceptual knowledge also involves norms for attentiveness, discrimination, unification, exclusion, and conceptual organization that do not function like physiological laws. And so (as Hegel says, "as a result") we should be said to stand always by them and yet also "beyond them." This can all still seem to introduce far too much normative variability into a process, perception, that seems all much more a matter of physiological fact. But while Hegel certainly accepts that the physiological components of perception are *distinguishable* from the norm-following or interpretive elements, he also insists that the physiological and the normative aspects are *inseparable* in perception itself. (As in Heidegger's phenomenology, there are not two stages to perception, as if a perception of a white rectangular solid is then "interpreted as" a refrigerator. What we *see* is a refrigerator.)

The second dimension of this claim from ¶80 concerns how such consciousness is "beyond itself" in another way. Besides the claim that consciousness, as he says, "negates" what it is presented with, that it does not merely take in but determines what is the case, the claim is also that ordinary, everyday consciousness is *always* "going beyond itself," never *wholly* absorbed in what it is attending to, never simply or only *in* a perceptual state, but always resolving its own conceptual activity; and this in a way that means it can be said both to be self-affirming, possibly issuing in judgments and imperatives, but also potentially "self-negating," aware that what it resolves or takes to be the case might not be the case. It somehow "stands above" what it also affirms, to use an image that Hegel sometimes invokes (although he again means: stands above *in* so resolving, not *in addition to*). It adds to the interpretive problems to cite below the canonical formulation of this point, but it might help us see how important it is for his whole position and why he is using language like "negativity" for *consciousness itself*. (Such terminology is the key *explicans* for his eventual claim that self-conscious consciousness is desire.) This formulation in Hegelese is from the "Phenomenology" section of the last version of his *Encyclopedia* (the "Berlin Phenomenology" again):

> The I is now this subjectivity, this infinite relation to itself, but therein, namely in this subjectivity, lies its negative relation to itself, diremption, differentiation, judgment. *The I judges, and this constitutes it as consciousness*; it repels itself from itself; this is a logical determination.[25]

So the large question to which Hegel thinks we have been brought by his account of consciousness in the first three chapters is: just *what is it* for a being to be not just a recorder of the world's impact on one's senses, but to be *for itself* in its engagements with objects? What is it in general *for a being to be for itself*, for "itself to be at issue for it in its relation with what is not it"? (This is the problem that arose with the "Kantian" revelation in the *Understanding* chapter of the PhG that, in trying to get to the real nature of the essence of appearances, "understanding experiences only itself," which, he says, raises the problem: "the cognition of *what consciousness knows in knowing itself* requires a still more complex

---

[25] BPhG, 2, my emphasis.

movement" [¶167, my emphasis].) This is the fundamental issue being explored in Chapter Four. That the basic structure of the Kantian account is preserved until this point is clear from the following:

> With that first moment, self-consciousness exists as *consciousness*, and the whole breadth of the sensuous world is preserved for it, but at the same time only as related to the second moment, the unity of self-consciousness with itself. (¶167)[26]

This passage and indeed all of ¶167 indicate that Hegel does have in mind a response to the problem of a self-conscious consciousness (of the whole breadth of the sensible world) developed in the first three chapters (what *is* the relation to itself inherent in any possible relation to objects?), and that he insists on a commonsense acknowledgment that whatever account we give of a self-determining self-consciousness, it is not a *wholly* autonomous or independent self-relating; the "sensuous world" must be preserved.

But it is at this point that he then suddenly makes a much more controversial, pretty much unprepared for, and not at all recognizably Kantian, claim:

> But this opposition between its appearance and its truth has only the truth for its essence, namely, the unity of self-consciousness with itself. This unity must become essential to self-consciousness, which is to say, self-consciousness is *desire* itself. (¶167)

Hegel is talking about an "opposition" between appearance and truth here because he has, in his own words, just

---

[26] Cf. again the *Berlin Phenomenology*: "In consciousness I am also self-conscious, but *only also*, since the object has a side in itself which is not mine" (BPhG, 56).

summarized the issue of consciousness's "negative" relation
to the world and itself this way:

> Otherness thereby exists for it *as a being*, that is, as a *distin-*
> *guished moment*, but, for it, it is also the unity of itself with
> this distinction as a *second distinguished* moment. (¶167)

That is, consciousness may be said to affirm implicitly a con-
strual of some intentional content, but since it has thereby
(by its own "taking") negated any putative immediate certainty, since it is also always "beyond itself," its eventual
"unity with itself," its satisfaction that what *it* takes to be the
case *is* the case and can be integrated with everything else it
takes to be the case, requires the *achievement* of a "unity with
itself," not any immediate certainty or self-regard. (This is
his echo of the Kantian point that the unity of apperception
must be achieved; contents must be, as Kant says, "brought"
to the unity of apperception.)

But still, at this point, the gloss he gives on the claim that
"self-consciousness is desire" is not much help. The gloss
is, as if an appositive, "This [the unity of self-consciousness
with itself] "must become essential to self-consciousness,
which is to say, etc." The first hint of a practical turn emerges
just here when Hegel implies that we need to understand
self-consciousness as *a unity* to be *achieved*, that there is some
"opposition" between self-consciousness and itself, a kind of
self-estrangement, which, he seems to be suggesting, we are
moved to overcome. The unity of self-consciousness with
itself "*muß ihm wesentlich werden*," must become essential to
the experiencing subject, a practical turn of phrase that in
effect almost unnoticed serves as the pivot around which the
discussion turns suddenly and deeply practical. (As we shall
see, this unity eventually does much more clearly "become
essential" as a result of a putative encounter with another
and opposing self-conscious being. And it is clearly practical

in the everyday sense in which we might say to someone, "You're wasting chances for advancement; your career must *become* essential to you.")

There would be no problem here, or not as much of one, if Hegel had just noted that human desire is self-conscious desire (something he also of course holds). That would be to make the point that self-conscious desirers do not desire in episodic and isolated moments of desire; they desire in the light of the other things they desire, for one thing, and that alone is a way of saying that the desire itself is self-conscious (and not that human desires are like animal desires but "then" can be also self-monitored). But Hegel's speculative "reverse" predication is what requires a deeper interpretation.

Since the self-conscious aspect of ordinary empirical consciousness is much more like a self-determination, or one could say a resolve or a committing oneself (what Fichte called a self-positing) than a simple self-observation or direct awareness, Hegel begins again to discuss consciousness as a "negation" of the world's independence and otherness. He means to say: we are, just in actively attending to the world, overcoming the indeterminacy, opacity, foreignness, potential confusion, and disconnectedness of what we are presented with by resolving what belongs together with what, tracking objects through changes and so forth.[27] Hegel

[27] Cf.

> The 'I' is as it were the crucible and fire which consumes the loose plurality of sense and reduces it to unity . . . The tendency of all man's endeavors is to understand the world, to appropriate and subdue it to himself; and to this end the positive reality of the world must be as it were crushed and pounded, in other words, idealized.

Enzyklopädie der philosophischen Wissenschaften, Erster Teil. Die Wissenschaft der Logik, in *Werke* (Frankfurt: Suhrkamp, 1969–79), Bd. 8, p. 118; *Hegel's Logic, Being Part One of the Encyclopedia of the Philosophical Sciences*, trans. W. Wallace (Oxford: Clarendon Press, 1982), p. 69.

then makes another unexpected move when he suggests that we consider the most uncomplicated and straightforward experience of just this striving or orectic for-itself-ness, what he calls "life":

> By way of this reflective turn into itself, the object has become *life*. What self-consciousness distinguishes from itself *as existing* also has in it, insofar as it is posited as existing, not merely the modes of sense-certainty and perception. It is being which is reflected into itself, and the object of immediate desire is something *living*. (¶168)

This is the most basic experience[28] of what it is to be at issue for oneself as one engages the world. As Hegel says, we begin with what we know we now need, a "being reflected into itself," and our question, how should we properly describe the self of the self-relation necessary for conscious intentionality and ultimately agency, is given the broadest possible referent, its own mere life. We have something like a sentiment of self as living and, as we shall see, as also needing to-be-achieved, requiring that the living being act purposively in order to live. Other objects too are not now merely external existents, "*not merely the modes of sense-certainty and perception*" (although they are *also* that) but, in order to move beyond the empty formality of "I am the I who is thinking these thoughts," they are now also considered as *objects for <u>the living subject</u>*, as threats to, means to, or indifferent to such life-sustaining. This brute or simple *for-itself* quality of living consciousness (which form of self-relation we share with animals) will not remain the focus of Hegel's interest for long, but, if it is becoming plausible that Hegel is indeed trying to extend the issue raised in the

[28] That is, the one that presupposes the least.

Consciousness section (and neither changing the subject, nor repeating the problem and desideratum in a figurative way), it already indicates what was just suggested: that he is moving quickly away from Kant's transcendental-formal account of the apperceptive nature of consciousness. The I is "for itself" in consciousness for Kant only in the sense that the I (whoever or whatever it is) must be able to accompany all my representations. The world is experienced as categorically ordered because I in some sense order it (I *think* it as such and such), and that activity is not merely triggered into operation by the sense contents of experience. I undertake it, but I do so only in the broad formal sense of temporally unifying, having a take on, the contents of consciousness, bringing everything under the unity of a formally conceived apperceptive I. (This simply means that every content must be such that *one continuous I can think it*.) The "I" *is* just the unity effected. The subject's relation to objects is a self-relation only in this sense, and Hegel has introduced what seems like a different and at first arbitrary shift in topics to my sustaining my own life as the basic or first or most primary model of this self-relation, not merely sustaining the distinction between, say, successions of representations and a representation of succession.

Now the whole section on life, essentially ¶168 to ¶174, is among the most opaque of any passages in Hegel (which is saying something). I should note that what I need here is Hegel's basic framework, in which he starts with the claim that with our "reflective turn" ("*durch diese Reflexion in sich selbst*") consciousness is related to "life." Self-relation as mere sentiment of oneself as living and as having to maintain life does not, however, establish my taking up and leading my determinate life as an individual. I am just an exemplar of the species requirements of my species, playing them out within the infinite "totality" of life itself as genus. Just by living I am nothing but a moment in the universal process of life, a kind of Schellingean universal (and Schelling talked this way about life). But throughout, the framework is: the first *object* of self-consciousness is life. That is, Hegel does not suddenly decide to talk about life, just qua life. As he says several times, he wants to understand life as the immediate object of desire (itself the most immediate form of self-relation), a sentiment of self that opens a gap, something negative to be filled (requiring the negation of barriers to life and the negation of stasis, in the face of the need to lead a life). That is, I take a main point to be that introduced in ¶168: in this self-relation, there is an "estrangement" (*Entzweiung*), "between self-consciousness and life," as he says. All through the phenomenology of "life as the infinite universal substance as the object of desire," the problem Hegel keeps pointing to is how, under what conditions, the self-relating can be said to become a relating to self that is a relation to *me*, a distinction within the universal genus, life. I seem rather just to be subject to the imperatives or demands of life for my species. *Rather than being the subject of my desires, I am subject to my desires.*

The first three chapters have already established the need to understand some sort of normative autonomy, and this first actuality of self-relatedness, life and leading a life, conflicts with this requirement unless such a subject can establish its independence from life. What is important to my account here is the course of this "becoming determinate" account until it begins to break into its conclusion, toward the end of ¶172, until "this estrangement of the undifferentiated fluidity is *the very positing of individuality*" ("*dies Entzweien der unterschiedlosen Flüssigkeit ist eben das Setzen der Individualität*"). Such a self-determined individual must be *established* and that especially requires a different, non-natural relation with another subject who must realize the same self-relatedness. This will be the subject of chapter 2. What Hegel struggles to say after this is why, without the inner mediation by the outer, that is, without a self-relation in relation to another self, this all fails, a typically Hegelian coming a cropper.[29]

This shift to the topic of life is also not arbitrary because Hegel has objected, and will continue to object through-out his career, to any view of the "I" in "I think" as such a merely formal indicator of "the I or he or it" (in Kant's phrase) which thinks. In Hegel's contrasting view, while we can certainly make a general point about the necessity for unity in experience by abstracting from any determination of such a subject and go on to explore the conditions of such unity, we will not get very far in specifying such conditions without, let us say, more determination already in the notion of the subject of experience. This criticism is tied to what was by far the most widespread dissatisfaction with Kant's first *Critique* (which Hegel shared) and which remains today one of its greatest weaknesses: the arbitrariness of Kant's Table of Categories, the fact that he has no way of deducing from "the 'I think' must be able to accompany all my repre-sentations" *what* the I must necessarily think, what forms it must employ, in thinking its representations. The emptiness of Kant's "I" is directly linked for Hegel to the ungrounded-ness and arbitrariness of his Table of Categories.[30]

---

[29] See the different account in Neuhouser, "Desire, Recognition, and the Relation between Bondsman and Lord," p. 43.
[30] Hegel's formulation of this point is given in ¶197 in his own inimi-table style.

> To *think* does not mean to think as an *abstract I*, but as an
> I which at the same time signifies *being-in-itself*, that is, it

However, understanding this charge would take us deep into Hegel's criticisms of Kantian formality. What we need now is a clearer sense of what Hegel is proposing, not so much what he is rejecting. Let me first complete a brief summary of the themes in Chapter Four (once we begin reading it this way) and then see where we are.

III

As we have seen, if a self-conscious consciousness is to be understood as striving in some way, then the most immediate embodiment of such a striving would be a self's attention to itself as a living being.[31] That is how it is immediately for

---

has the meaning of being an object in its own eyes, or of conducting itself vis-à-vis the objective essence in such a way that its meaning is that of the *being-for-itself* of that consciousness for which it is.

[31] This is relevant to another broad point. Hegel's is not a genetic account; there is no matter-of-historical-fact development from a merely conscious state to a self-consciously conscious one. But the "phenomenologically" developmental structure of the PhG helps highlight that no one ever simply *is* apperceptively conscious just as such (at least not without a distorting, extreme abstraction similar to Kant's insistence on formality). One is apperceptively conscious in some structural way or other, open to challenges in one way and not another, "beyond itself" in one way rather than another. If apperceptive consciousness is ultimately to be the maker of claims for which one is responsible, then one must be in a position to redeem them and in that sense being such an apperceptive subject always involves, commits one to, the achievement of such redemption in some way rather than another. This can be more or less successful, and so the achievement can be more or less realized. (And until modernity, in Hegel's account, such a realization was almost wholly implicit, barely realized.) Although it is clearly possible on the logical level to distinguish capacity and realization, Hegel is forever going on about the distortions that result from strictly separating questions of the content of some capacity (say,

itself in relation to other objects. Living beings, like animals, do not exist in the way non-living beings (like rocks or telephones) *merely* exist; they must strive to stay alive, and so we have our first example of the desideratum, a self-relation in relation to objects. Life must be led, sustained, and this gap between my present life and what I must do to sustain it in the future is what is meant by calling consciousness *desire* as lack or gap, and so a negation of objects as impediments or mere things.[32] If consciousness and desire can be linked as closely as Hegel wants to (that is, identified), then consciousness is not an isolatable registering and responding capacity of the living being that is conscious. And if this all

---

"justifiability") from realization, as in the first paragraph of the *Philosophy of Right*, for example. "The subject matter of the philosophical science of right is the Idea of right—the concept of right and its actualization." *Elements of the Philosophy of Right*, ed. A. Wood, trans. H. Nisbet (Cambridge: Cambridge University Press, 1991), p. 28.

It may help establish the plausibility of this reading by noting how much this practical conception of normativity and intentionality was in the air at the time. I have already indicated how indebted this chapter is to Fichte. Ludwig Siep has clearly established how much Hegel borrowed from Fichte for the later sections on recognition and for his practical philosophy in general. See his *Anerkennung als Prinzip der praktischen Philosophie* (Alber: Freiburg/Munich, 1979) and many of the important essays in *Praktische Philosophie im deutschen Idealismus* (Frankfurt a.M.: Surhkamp, 1992).

[32] Readers of Peirce will recognize here his category of "Secondness." As in "you have a sense of resistance and at the same time a sense of effort. . . . They are only two ways of describing the same experience. It is a double consciousness. We become aware of ourself [sic] by becoming aware of the not-self." C. S. Peirce, *Collected Papers of Charles Sanders Peirce*, vols. I–VI, ed. Charles Hartshorne and Paul Weiss (Cambridge, Mass.: Harvard University Press, 1931–35), I, p. 324. An excellent exploration of the links between pragmatism and Hegel: Richard Bernstein, *Praxis and Action* (Philadelphia: University of Pennsylvania Press, 1971).

can be established, then we will at this step have moved far away from considering a self-conscious consciousness as a kind of self-aware spectator of the passing show and moved closer to considering it as an engaged, practical being, whose practical satisfaction of desire is essential to understanding the way the world originally makes sense to it (the way it makes sense of the world), or is intelligible at all. Hegel's claim is that consciousness *is* desire, not merely that it is accompanied by desire. (Obviously this claim has some deep similarities with the way Heidegger insists that *Dasein*'s unique mode of being-in-the-world is *Sorge*, or care, and with Heidegger's constant insistence that this has nothing to do with a subject projecting its pragmatic concerns onto a putatively neutral, directly apprehended content.)

At points Hegel tries to move away from very general and abstract points about living beings and desire and to specify the distinctive character of desire that counts as "self-consciousness," as was claimed in his identification. He wants, that is, to distinguish actions that are merely the natural expression of desire (and a being that is merely subject to its desires), and a corresponding form of self-consciousness that is a mere sentiment of self, from actions undertaken in order to satisfy a desire, the actions of a being that does not just embody its self-sentiment but can be said to act *on* such a self-conception. He wants to distinguish natural or animal desire from human desire and so tries to distinguish a cycle of desires and satisfactions that continually arise and subside in animals from beings *for whom* their desires can be objects of attention, issues at stake, ultimately *reasons* to be acted on or not. This occurs in a very rapid series of transitions in ¶175 where Hegel starts distinguishing the cycle of the urges and satisfactions of mere desire from a satisfaction that can confirm the genuinely self-relating quality of consciousness, rather than its mere self-sentiment.[33]

That is, we have already seen a crucial aspect of the structure of Hegel's account: that any self-relating is always also in a way provisional and a projecting outward, beyond the near immediacy of any mere self-taking. Conscious takings of any sort are defeasible, held open as possibilities, and so must be tested; and avowed commitments must be realized in action for there to be any realization of the avowed intention (and so revelation of what the subject was in fact committed to doing). The projected self-sentiment of a merely living self is *realized* by the "negation" of the object of desire necessary for life, part of an endless cycle of being subject to one's desires and satisfying them. This all begins to change at the end of the paragraph (¶175), as Hegel contemplates a distinct kind of object which in a sense "*negates back*," and not merely in the manner of a prey that resists a predator, but which can also, as he says, "effect this negation in itself"; or, come to be in the self-relation required by our desiring self-consciousness. That is, Hegel introduces into the conditions of the "satisfaction" of any self-relating another self-consciousness, an object that cannot merely be destroyed or negated in the furtherance of life without the original self-consciousness losing its confirming or satisfying moment.

---

[33] Eventually, at a certain stage in his argument, Hegel (and I) will begin referring to "desire" as an ellipsis for distinctly human desire, whereas he starts off with a merely "animal" notion of desire, something already suggested by the somewhat cruder word, *Begierde* (not *Begheren*, for example). The context should make clear the different uses, with an occasional reminder to make clear that he thinks there is something qualitatively different about human desire, and that a major point of his phenomenology is to make that distinction clear.

He then identifies a further condition for this distinction that is perhaps the most famous claim in the *Phenomenology*.

It is this one. "Self-consciousness attains its satisfaction only in another self-consciousness" (¶175). He specifies this in an equally famous passage from ¶178. "Self-consciousness exists *in* and *for itself* because and by way of its existing in and for itself for an other; i.e., it exists only as recognized."

As we shall see in more detail in the analysis of this claim in the next chapter, Hegel wants to introduce a complication into any account of the self-relation he is trying to show is constitutive for intentional consciousness and purposive deeds. As we have seen, consciousness is said to be "beyond itself" because its self-relating self-determining is always defeasible (or challengeable in the case of action) and so its being in its very self-relation in some way "held open" to such a possibility is considered a constitutive condition. In the broadest sense this means that such takings and doings are supported by reasons, even if mostly in deeply implicit and rarely challenged ways. (Conscious takings can always "rise" to the level of explicit judgments and defenses of judgments; habitual actions can be defended if necessary.) Hegel now introduces the possibility—unavoidable given the way he has set things up—that all such considerations are uniquely open to challenge by other conscious, acting beings. Such challenges could initially be considered as merely more natural obstacles in the way of desire-satisfaction in all the various forms now at issue in Hegel's account. But by considering imaginatively the possibility of a challenge that forces the issue to the extreme (where attachment to life and mere subjection to desire can be said to become an *option*), a "struggle to the death," Hegel tries to show how the unique nature of such a challenge from another like-minded being forces the issue of the normative

(or not just naturally explicable) character of one's takings
and practical commitments, and any possible response, to
the forefront. To be norm-sensitive at all is then shown not
just to be *open* to these unique sorts of challenges, but to
be finally *dependent* on some resolution of them. It is on
the basis of this account, how we can be shown to open
ourselves to such challenges and such dependence just as
a result of a "phenomenological" consideration of the implications of the apperception thesis, that Hegel begins his
attempt to establish one of the most ambitious claims of
the *Phenomenology of Spirit*: the sociality of consciousness
and action.

IV

Before concluding this chapter, let me pause here to consider
both the objections John McDowell has made to this sort of
reading and his alternative interpretation. He says that in
the crucial *Begierde* passage of ¶167, "There is no suggestion here of anything as specific as a mode of consciousness
that has its objects in view only in so far as they can be seen
as conducive or obstructive to its purposes,"[34] and he says
that my reading takes the notion of desire "too literally." My
response is of course that there is no question of a more
or less literal understanding; that by using the word desire,
Hegel simply means to introduce the topic of desire as a
continuation of his discussion of consciousness, and goes on
in that register, discussing life as the object of desire, the
conflict between desiring beings, and ultimately the impossibility of understanding a subject's relation to itself and the

[34] McDowell, AI, p. 38.

world apart from that subject's relation to other subjects.[35] McDowell's argument against this reading is for the most part comprised of an alternate reading that he suggests is more plausible.

But his reading also depends on a Hegelian reading of Kant's Transcendental Deduction, and we should start there, as he does at the beginning of his Lordship and Bondage article. Kant wants to argue that the categories are objectively valid (that there is synthetic a priori knowledge) by arguing that the categories, while subjective conditions for the possible thinkability of any possible object in experience, are also a "condition under which every intuition must stand in order to become an object for me" (B138). If he can show this, he can show that categorical order is not merely "imposed" on an intuited manifold. To show this adequately (which for McDowell (and Hegel and me) he only begins to do in the second-edition deduction), he must forestall the objection that while one might argue that objects, considered as objects of thought (of judgment) must conform to categorical conditions for unity, it is quite conceivable that the conditions of their simple givenness to sensibility might *not* be *those* categorical conditions of unity. McDowell thinks Kant goes off track here by setting out to prove something *like* this desideratum (but not this) in trying to prove that

[35] This way of talking about self-consciousness as itself a matter of desire is not unique to the Jena PhG or the so-called early Hegel. Very late, in the BPhG, he puts the point this way:

> As this self-certainty with regard to the object, abstract self-consciousness therefore constitutes *the drive to posit* what it is implicitly; i.e. to give content and objectivity to the abstract knowledge of itself, and, conversely, to free itself from its sensuousness, to sublate the given objectivity, and to posit the identity of this objectivity with itself. (BPhG, 59, my emphasis)

for *our* intuitional conditions (space and time as subjective forms), this possible contrast could not take place, there could not be objects given *under such subjective conditions* discordant with what the understanding requires. This appeal to our subjective forms then for McDowell "subjectifies" or idealizes the result and proves the results true only of "phenomena," given these quasi-factual, peculiar-to-humans forms of sensibility. McDowell (and Hegel and I) want to eliminate this sort of species-specific "restriction."

How might one do that? One might just directly analyze or separate out criteria, the absence of which would permit no distinction between what appears to be the case and what is, thereby rendering experience of a determinate object impossible. One criterion might be the differentiability between the successive perceptions of parts of something that in fact exist all simultaneously. We could be said to find that such a distinction is necessary and then show that our categorical conditions allow us to make it, and thus have demonstrated the right "equipoise" as McDowell calls it, between objective and subjective. As he puts it, "To hold that the very idea of objectivity can be understood only as part of such a [subjective] structure is not to abandon the independently real in favor of projections from subjectivity."[36]

If at this point someone were *still* to complain that we were still proving only that we need this distinction, not that objects must exhibit it, we could respond somewhat in the way Hegel does in his Introduction: this is on the verge of

---

[36] McDowell, AI, p. 37. It is an odd way to put the point, but one might say that what one gets when one applies Hegel's suggestions about how to interpret what is going on in the second edition deduction, all understood as a way to avoid a subjective idealism, is something very like Strawson's interpretation of the *Critique* in *The Bounds of Sense* (London: Methuen, 1966).

asking that we consider what the world is, but apart from any way we have of knowing it. Without the distinction in question, the notion of an object in experience is incoherent, full stop.

This is the background of what McDowell calls his "heterodox" reading of the self-consciousness chapter of the PhG. And a good deal of what he says fits many passages. It often can seem as if one were considering a single subject as an object of analysis, as if struggling to formulate properly the right equipoise or balance between the free exercises of apperceptive intelligence and that same subject's empirical dependence and receptivity. Such a dependence could first be conceived as some "other" to such a self-consciousness, constraining it exogenously, even through the subject's own sensibility. But then consciousness could be said "to realize" that such a putative other was, as Hegel puts it, *itself another self-consciousness*, not a passive or merely receptive "other," that such a sensible dimension was an aspect *of its own* self-conscious relation to the world. This would all be presented as if a kind of theatrical Hegelian "acting out" of Kant's famous footnote at B160n.,[37] where he apparently blurs his

[37] The note to B160 reads:

> Space, represented as object (as we are required to do in geometry) contains more than mere form of intuition; it also contains combination of the manifold, given according to the form of sensibility, in an intuitive representation, so that the form of intuition gives only a manifold, the formal intuition gives unity of representation. In the Aesthetic I have treated this unity as belonging merely to sensibility, simply in order to emphasize that it precedes any concept, although as a matter of fact it presupposes a synthesis which does not belong to the senses but through which all concepts of space and time first become possible.

own intuition-understanding duality. In a similar but more dramatic and figurative way, Hegel could be said to begin to break down the strict opposition between the conditions of an apperceptive understanding and a *distinct*, separable form of sensible intuition. In his own inimitable way, he could be said to be doing this by portraying that struggle as at first a negation and disowning and refusal so extreme as to be a kind of attempt to "kill off" its own life (the struggle to death for recognition), then by subjugating it (the relation of lord and bondsman), then by a slow and gradual realization of its identity (as self-conscious subject) with what it has attempted to negate and dominate.[38]

Further, it is certainly true, as McDowell says, that there remains a deep "structural" issue at stake (remains, that is, from the first three chapters). Hegel is continuing to try to show why the "negation" of the object's otherness cannot be simple annihilation (or in our Kantian language "subjective imposition"), whether the object is an external or an internal object. Such an other must be *aufgehoben*, preserved as well as negated, but again McDowell interprets all of this as

---

[38] A point in McDowell's favor: as Hegel continues the discussion beyond the relation of Lord and Bondsman, the focus seems to be on *intra*-psychic consolations grasped at by an alienated self: stoicism, skepticism, and the unhappy consciousness. A point against it: these all seem to be consolations required *because* of the unsatisfying character of the *social* positions of opposed self-consciousnesses. Another point in favor: the transition out of the section on self-consciousness returns straightaway to reason's relation to the *world*, in this case, "reason's certainty of finding itself" in the world. For me a point against it is that this putative sufficiency of reason as such (another consolation strategy) *fails*, requiring, in a kind of repetition (in the Chapter Five–Chapter Six relation) of the Consciousness-Self-Consciousness transition, the move to a practical and socially contested notion of rational authority at the end of Chapter Five and again in Chapter Six.

an intra-psychic issue, where the latter issue remains self-consciousness's proper relation to itself, and especially to the deliverances of its own sensible faculties. This all correctly isolates what McDowell calls the structure at issue in the discussion, but I think it unnecessarily formalizes and so dilutes what Hegel is talking about, such that desire, life, and negation get purchase in McDowell's account only as exemplifications of structure (although, again, to be sure, he is certainly right that they are *also* that). As far as I can see, on McDowell's reading, Hegel is extending and developing with several figures, exemplifications, and illustrations, and even "allegories," the desiderata we now know we need at the conclusion of the first three chapters. In its own terms, this advances Hegel's argument as it further clarifies, even dramatizes, what is required in any such potential equipoise, but I have already tried to indicate why I think the issue cannot be isolated as a drama going on within one consciousness.

That is, even in the interpretation of the intra-psychic issue McDowell is considering, I think that Hegel has already set things up so that self-consciousness cannot, let us say, find itself (*or* its "unity" or its "equipoise" with the deliverances of its sensibility) "inside itself." The self-relation in relation to an object that has emerged as a topic from the first three chapters is not a relation to an object of any kind, and so involves no grasp of anything. (The subject of the world is not, that is, any kind of object *in the world*.) When Hegel had declared that in the understanding's relation of objects the understanding discovers only itself, it would distort his understanding of what has been achieved to import the model of consciousness in any sense, whatever equipoise is suggested between subject and object in consciousness. According to Hegel, such a self-regard is always transparent and a projection "outward," and therein lies the essential negative or going-beyond-itself moment in Hegel's account. In reporting what I think (even to myself), I am not reporting anything about me, but what I take to be true. In being aware of what I desire, of a desirous me, I am not reporting an affective state but thereby avowing a possible project of action in the world,[39] and it is in the world that the natural cycle of desire or need and satisfaction will be, later in the account, interrupted in a way of decisive importance for the rest of the PhG.

I want to talk about such sociality in the next chapter, but to anticipate, McDowell complains that when Hegel makes his well-known claim in ¶175 that "self-consciousness achieves its satisfaction only in another self-consciousness," he cannot mean to begin describing an encounter with another person because that would leave the original puzzlement still a puzzle. That problem was, in Hegelese, *the otherness of the sensible world* and how to overcome it (in the simple sense know it, but without turning it into an idea). All that seems bypassed, he thinks, if we treat "another self-consciousness" as a second person. "What has happened to 'the whole expanse of the sensible world'?"[40] McDowell asks. He therefore concludes that "another self-consciousness" in "self-consciousness achieves its satisfaction only in another self-consciousness," must still be referring to a singular self-consciousness, now aware of itself as self-conscious, and in *that* sense other to itself.[41]

[39] Only "possible" because I can obviously have desires I would not think of trying to satisfy.
[40] McDowell, AI, p. 41.
[41] So to state the disagreement as clearly as I can, when Hegel says in ¶177, glossing his claim that "*A self-consciousness exists for a self-consciousness*," that "only thereby does self-consciousness in fact exist, for

But Hegel has always been clear that he is interested throughout in a self-relation *in relation to objects*. That problem has not disappeared. It is in the background everywhere and has been reformulated in terms of the objects of desire for a living, desiring self-conscious consciousness. And Hegel specifically alerts us that we should not think of the whole expanse of the sensible world, although still "there," *in the same way as before*:

> What self-consciousness distinguishes from itself *as existing* also has in it, insofar as it is posited as existing, *not merely the modes of sense-certainty and perception*. It is being which is reflected into itself, and the object of immediate desire is something *living*. (¶168, my emphasis)

This seems clearly to say that the new "object" of consciousness will be itself (as discovered in the Understanding chapter) but not as observed object, rather as "life." So its relation to the world will be as a self-related living being to objects for life. And there is no reason to think that his early formulation will remain Hegel's last word. The problem of the status of the sensible world in consciousness's self-relation in relation to an object will recur again, formulated at a higher level, in the discussion of Observing Reason, in the first half of Chapter Five of the PhG. In this chapter, having shown phenomenologically the

---

it is only therein that the unity of itself in its otherness comes to be for it," McDowell takes this to mean that only by understanding the subject-object relation in terms of, let us say, the logic of self-consciousness in its dependence and independence, will we understand "the unity of itself in *its* otherness" that we have been looking for since Chapter One. I am arguing that Hegel is claiming that the relation between subject and sensible object always generates a "dissatisfaction" that can only be resolved in the relation between a subject and other such subjects.

necessity of an account of such a self-relation, Hegel is concentrating mainly on that. He has not forgotten the sensory world.[42]

Finally and briefly, McDowell takes on the toughest passage for his reading, ¶177, where Hegel says that in this chapter the "concept [*Begriff*] of spirit is already present for us," that "a self-consciousness exists for a self-consciousness" (I note that Hegel says *ein* Selbstbewusstsein exists for *ein* Selbstbewusstsein, although McDowell could claim that our putatively disunified subject is *so* disunified at this point that its other self can appear to it *as* another self,

---

[42] There is a very clear formulation of what McDowell is worried about in a later paper, a response to Stephen Houlgate's criticism of McDowell's interpretation of the Self-Consciousness chapter. McDowell says the following:

> My reading, now, is controlled by this thought: surely in this development Hegel cannot mean to have simply abandoned the form in which the antithesis first appeared, as an antithesis between empirically accessible reality and the subject consciousness. The object moment in the double object, which appears, after this development, as a living self-consciousness, must somehow stand in for the object moment as it figured in the first appearance of the antithesis, where it was "the whole expanse of the sensible world." Otherwise how can an *Aufhebung* of the antithesis, in the form in which it now appears, be a way to achieve what Hegel described as the movement of self-consciousness, at the beginning of the chapter? (*Owl of Minerva*, forthcoming)

What I am trying to show, as indicated previously, is that Hegel is arguing that the entire logic of the mind-world relation changes on "consciousness's" discovery in the Understanding chapter that its true object, what it is in fact knowing, is itself. And that relation (to itself) in its relation to the world is then shown to change in the presence of another subject. Hegel is not changing the subject, but continuing his exploration of the conditions for object-intentionality.

in a kind of epistemic schizophrenia).[43] In a famous phrase, Hegel here signals the arrival on the phenomenological scene of an "I that is a we and a we that is an I." McDowell says two things about this. One is that in this remark about spirit being present for us, Hegel makes clear that by "spirit" he merely means (at this point) an object that "is just as much I as object," that we have left behind an objectifying notion of a self or subject. Another is that Hegel could be read as just previewing coming attractions, noting the full phenomenology of *Geist*'s experience of itself will come later.[44]

It is true that Hegel stresses here that the self of self-consciousness is not an object, but first, Hegel in the full quotation says, "Because a self-consciousness is the object

[43] This is what he does say in correspondence:

> But it's part of the point of my reading that the indepen-dence-affirming self-consciousness begins by thinking *two* self-consciousnesses are in play. (Its concern is to affirm its independence; the supposedly other consciousness is depen-dent; it can't see how independence and dependence could be combined in one consciousness.) The reading would be pointless if it were supposed to be clear in advance that there's only one self-consciousness in play.

And in his response to Houlgate, he writes:

> The *pathological* self-conceptions whose implications con-sciousness is working through, in those stretches of its "experience," are captured *figuratively* by the images of the struggle to the death and the master's relation to the slave. (my emphasis, *Owl of Minerva*, forthcoming)

I find the surface details of the allegory confusing: that Hegel is por-traying a single subject so "*pathologically*" resistant to its sensible depen-dence that, in a kind of schizophrenic frenzy, it can be said to attempt to kill or obliterate such dependence in itself. *Why* would the "antithesis" consciousness experiences between its apperceptive intelligence and its object-dependent sensibility prompt such a radical, even "pathological" self-diremption?

[44] McDowell, AI, p. 42.

[of a self-consciousness], "the object is just as much an I as it is an object."

In the context of the passage, it does not seem possible to me to read this (¶177) as saying that self-consciousness has *itself* as an object of reflection, that no reference to another self-consciousness need be meant. (Note again the use of "ein Selbstbewusstsein," not just Selbstbewusstsein or "das Selbstbewusstsein.") That might be a possible reading if one frames the issue exclusively in terms of the preceding paragraph, ¶176. But a transition has already occurred in the text by this point. In ¶175 Hegel has already argued that the model of "mind and world," let us say, or "subject and object" in his terminology, obscures rather than helps reveal the nature of the self-consciousness essential to consciousness. On this model, desire is a manifestation of a natural process, and no true orectic intentionality has been achieved:

> Self-consciousness is thus unable by way of its negative relation to the object to sublate it, and for that reason it once again to an even greater degree re-engenders the object as well as the desire. (¶175)

This claim serves as the premise of his inference to a radically *new* "object":

> On account of the self-sufficiency of the object, it thus can only achieve satisfaction if *this object itself effects the negation* in it [the object]; and the object must in itself effect this negation of itself, for it is *in itself* the negative, and it must be for the other what it is. Since the object is the negation in itself and at the same time is therein self-sufficient, it is consciousness. (my emphasis)

This seems clearly to say that this negation must be "reflected" back to self-consciousness in order to be successful or satisfying; that one's claim for example should not just produce submissive assent, but be *acknowledged* as authoritative. An object, or self-consciousness itself on its own (or within itself) cannot accomplish this, cannot achieve the unity that "must become essential to it." Hence the famous conclusion: "*Self-consciousness attains its satisfaction only in another self-consciousness.*"

Further, McDowell offers no explanation of why Hegel would gloss *that* claim ("the object is just as much an I as it is an object") by saying that spirit, *Geist*, which certainly *does* mean some sort of communal conception of subjectivity, should be a gloss on *that* passage.[45] Such a communal Geist, moreover, is not *just* said to be something to be discussed later. It *is* "vorhanden," here *now*. How could he say that on McDowell's interpretation?

Actually, ¶177 is not the most difficult passage for McDowell's interpretation. That honor goes to ¶182:

> In this way, this movement of self-consciousness in its relation to another self-consciousness has been represented as *the activity of one self-consciousness*, but this activity on the part of one self-consciousness has itself the twofold significance of being equally *its own activity* as well as *the other's activity*, for the other is likewise self-sufficient . . . Each sees *the other* do the same as what he himself does; each himself does what he demands of the other and for that reason also does what he does *only* insofar as the other does the same. A one-sided activity would be useless

---

[45] McDowell cites paragraphs ¶17 and ¶790 where Hegel does talk about substance and subject, object and subject at the same time, but neither can be offered as evidence of an alternate or early definition of *Geist*. I think that Hegel means what he says when he says that there is at hand *here*: an I that is a we and a we that is an I.

because what is supposed to happen can only be brought about by way of both of them bringing it about. (¶182)

I suppose it is possible to continue to claim that Hegel is still here talking about two aspects of a single self-consciousness, whether apperceptive and empirical I, or a subject discovering itself as not object but subject, and that language like "each sees *the other* do the same as what he himself does" remains "allegorical," but I think there is much more textual and systematic evidence to support a non-allegorical reading than the evidence McDowell cites.

V

So where does all this leave us? In general we have a picture of a self or subject of experience and action estranged from, or divided within itself (without, as Hegel put it, a "unity" that "must become essential to it") but conceived now in a way very different from Plato's divided soul, divided among distinct "parts" in competition for rule of the soul as a whole, and in a way very different both from other forms of metaphysical dualism, and from what would become familiar as the Freudian mind, split between the conscious and the distinct unconscious mind, or most explicitly for Hegel (and for Schiller) in distinction from the Kantian conception of noumenal and phenomenal selves. In a way somewhat similar to, and in an unacknowledged way in debt to Rousseau, Hegel treats this division *as a result*, not in any factual historical sense but as a disruption of natural orectic unity that must always already have resulted, and can only be rightly understood as effected. This division functions in Hegel as it does in some others as the source of the incessant desire not for rule or successful repression but for the wholeness so often the subject of broader philosophical reflections on human life. Hegel does not accept the Platonic or Cartesian or Kantian account of a fixed dualism and so entertains this aspiration for a genuine reconciliation of sorts within such divisions. This is so in Hegel because he does not treat this division as a matter of metaphysical fact. The problem of unity emerges not because of any discovery of a matter of fact divided soul, but in the light of the realization that what counts as an aspect of my agency and what an impediment to it or what is a constraint on freedom, is a different issue under different conditions. In this light, under the conditions Hegel entertains in this chapter, the natural cycle of desire and satisfaction is interrupted in a way for which there is not an immediate or natural solution, and one's status as subject, judge, agent, is now said to emerge, in varying degrees, imagined under a variety of those possible conditions, as a result of this putative unavoidable conflict. The premise for this account is the one we saw much earlier. Hegel's way of putting it was that consciousness must always be thought to be "beyond itself"; more expansively put: that we have to understand a human self-relation as always also a projection outward as much as a turn inward. Once we understand such a self-relation as a normative self-determination, such a self is open, opens itself to, counter-claim, contestation, refusal, a different form of negation that forces a different sort of response, what Hegel will describe as initially a struggle for recognition.

This is a lot to get by reflection on Kant's central idea, that "the 'I think' must be able to accompany all my representations," but that is, I have argued, Hegel's source. It is this reflection on Kantian spontaneity, understood by Hegel as also a self-dividing or self-alienating, that grounds the hope for an effected or resultant form of reconciliation of self with other, and thereby self with self.

This way of looking at things is the source of his most beautiful image for this aspect of his project, an image that (typically) resonates both with Christian and pagan undertones. Later in the PhG (¶669), he describes human existence itself as a "wound" ("*Wunde*"), but one which, he says, has been self-inflicted and which (one infers, which *therefore*) can be healed, even "without scars" ("*ohne Narben*"). Such a healing requires the resolution of the social dialectic that he introduces in the next phase of the argument of Chapter Four, and that will be our subject in the next chapter.

Chapter Two

On Hegel's Claim That "Self-Consciousness Finds Its Satisfaction Only in Another Self-Consciousness"

I

You all at this moment know what you are doing—reading a book about Hegel, let us say—and, as Elizabeth Anscombe among others made famous, you know it not by observation (the way you would know that someone else is reading something) nor by inference from observation. You know it just *by* engaging in such activity and sustaining that activity. Likewise, you know what you believe I mean to be saying without inspecting some mental inventory of your beliefs or any other mental items. You know it by knowing what you take me to be saying. Likewise, "knowing" what you are now doing would make no sense to you, would not be knowledge, unless the activity also seemed explicable; knowing what you are about involves knowing why you are about it, and so involves what you take to be the reasons you are doing it. Likewise, knowing what you believe involves knowing why you take something to be true, what you take to be reasons for believing it. No one, that is, "just" believes something or "just" does something.

What do these simple observations tell us about "self-consciousness"? I have argued that Hegel means to say something very similar and that, for Hegel, the claims make clear that self-consciousness is not the awareness of an object, at least not any observed object, and that it is a dynamic process, a doing in a way and a thinking in a way, not any momentary, second-order awareness. Somewhat surprisingly, he called that whole process "desire" and I suggested in the last chapter that this was because, looking at things this way, such a way of knowing oneself in knowing or doing anything, not being momentary or punctuated in time, must involve some projection over time, a way of constantly and implicitly being attentive to, or at least open to the possibility of, whether one had it right, either about what one believed to be true, or about what one was doing or whether one had the reasons one took oneself to have. This is, I think, the most important *aperçu* in what we call German Idealism and it receives its fullest expression in Hegel's thought. (The formulation just used was closer to the way Fichte would put the point in his discussion not of *Begierde* or desire but of *Streben* or striving.) I can put the same point another way, and at a very high altitude, by noting something unusual about Kant.

In what is known as the First Introduction to his last *Critique*, *Critique of Judgment*, Kant presented a very ambitious summary of his understanding of the basic human capacities involved in our knowing, doing, or feeling anything. He divided these capacities into three components, listing first what he called the basic "faculties of the mind," and then to each basic faculty, he assigned what he called a "higher cognitive faculty," something like the higher expression of such a faculty. So, to the basic "cognitive faculty," he assigned "understanding" as the higher faculty; to the basic capacity to feel pleasure and pain he assigned as its higher counterpart the faculty of judgment (as in aesthetic pleasure and aesthetic judgment). And then, in a move somewhat at odds with the standard picture of Kant's philosophy, he listed as our third basic capacity "desire" (*Begehrensvermögen*) and assigned to it as the expression of its higher cognitive faculty, "reason."[1]

Why would he make such a connection? I want to say that it is because for Kant reason is not a mere calculative faculty, as if a tool to be applied in the realization of ends. Rather, in the simplest sense, to be a creature with rational responsiveness is to be a creature that expects, demands, wants, struggles for justification, warrant, a righteousness both intellectual and moral; or, put another way, it is to feel a lack when such a justification is lacking. In his most familiar formulation of the point, to be a creature of reason is to be *unable* to rest content with knowledge of the mere "conditioned," but to seek to ascend always to knowledge of the "unconditioned." (Kant noted that even the demonstration by his critical philosophy that such knowledge was impossible would have no effect on such yearning and the continuation of such quests.)[2] Reason, he put it in another context, must be said to have its own "interests," its

---

[1] He also assigned to each "a priori principles." These were, respectively, "lawfulness, purposiveness, and obligation,'" and to each he assigned a "product," respectively: "nature, art and morality." *Kritik der Urteilskraft*, in *Gesammelte Schriften*, ed. Königlich Preussischen Akademie der Wissenschaften (Berlin: de Gruyter, 1922), Bd. V, p. 198.

[2] Indeed, even the resolutely prosaic Kant was inspired to use a variation of an erotic image: "We shall always return to metaphysics as to a beloved one with whom we have had a quarrel" (A850/B878).

own teleological structure clearly evident when we act and know that we are acting in one way rather than another, inspiring in all such cases the need for justification, especially to others (for Kant, to all others). It was this structure that would provide the basis for Kantian morality. One could put the point in the Hegelian terms framed in the first chapter: to be such a reason-responsive creature is to be self-related in this erotic way in relation to all objects to be known and actions to be carried out, to be, as Hegel said in his peculiar way, "beyond oneself." And what else is this sort of self-relation, so described—a striving, inability to rest content, all in a uniquely reason-sensitive way— but "desire"?

The philosophical trajectory in German Idealism that I am attempting to trace out and follow in these chapters is inspired by the spirit of Kant's classification, but it is difficult to explain in detail and when explained at all becomes immediately highly controversial. The summary of Hegel's claim would simply be that the phenomenon at the heart of this philosophical movement—self-consciousness—must be understood as a *practical* phenomenon in somewhat the same way that Kant's classification already indicates his own formulation of the priority of practical over theoretical reason. As we have seen, in Hegel this means that, given the proper understanding of what a self is, any self-relating, self-ascription, or self-avowal cannot be understood by treating a self-relation as a relation to any sort of object or by treating the relation as any sort of two-place intentional or introspectively observational relation. Instead, any such self-relation must be understood as something provisional and has to involve something to-be-achieved. The key historical figure in this post-Kantian development is Fichte, who understood the force of this point and its many implications better than almost anyone else.[3] But in the case of Hegel, the controversy and difficulty begin when we try to read his presentation of this point in his 1807 *Phenomenology of Spirit* in a way that fits into the flow of that text as a whole, and that means in a way that can explain how the discussion of self-consciousness as desire, or in the topic for this chapter, the discussion of self-conscious satisfaction in another self-consciousness is, as it appears to be, a continuous development of the first three chapters, and that means a continuation of the discussion of varieties of putatively direct mind-world relations.

II

My suggestion throughout has been that we take our bearings again from Kant, who began this trajectory by arguing that any possible objective purport in experience (any intentional determinacy, the possibility that thought could be of objects at all) has to be understood as a relation that must be actively established, cannot be understood as a result only of sensory interchange with the world, as if the mere presence of sensible objects and their modification of sensibility on its own, as it were, sets or triggers the content of conscious thought. This is what Kant meant by claiming that all contentful consciousness is apperceptive, a self-relation in relation to objects. In the broadest sense this simply means that perceptual knowledge of something like a book on the

---

[3] Fichte also had quite a lot to say about the issue in this chapter, recognition, from which Hegel borrowed freely. But Fichte discussed recognition for the most part only in a legal and to some degree moral context, as the appropriate relation between free and rational individuals.

table involves in some way not easy to spell out my "taking" there to be a book on the table, and not just *my coming to be in a book-perceiving state*. (Wilfrid Sellars, in his classic essay, "Empiricism and the Philosophy of Mind," made this point by saying that perception is "so to speak, making an assertion or claim.")[4] It is not easy to spell this out because the character of the conceptual activity at work is difficult to describe. As noted before, it certainly does not mean that experience actually consists of some string of impossibly many explicit judgments. But the key point is that any conscious attentiveness to content of a sort cannot be said merely to happen to a subject in any subject's experience, but must be a taking, an exercise of what Kant called spontaneity, even if not an exercise attended to as such. This point, that it must be such an active taking, is what Kant means by saying that consciousness is itself apperceptive. (At any point when there is some need to do so, a challenge or an anomaly, any such taking can always be made into a judgment; it is always available for such an explicit claim.) That is, in all my conscious attentiveness to the world there is some kind of self-relating going on, an implicit attention to the normative dimensions of all experience, an openness we might say everywhere and always to whether I am getting it right, an openness that must be "held open," all as a characteristic of my attentiveness. It is this feature of that attentiveness that for Kant and his successors forever makes a wholly psychologistic or naturalistic account of consciousness incomplete.

In the last chapter I tried to show how Hegel argued that properly understanding this point required us to think of

---

[4] Wilfrid Sellars, *Empiricism and the Philosophy of Mind* (Cambridge, Mass.: Harvard University Press, 1997), p. 39.

such self-consciousness as always in a way provisional, as opening up a kind of gap between a subject's initial resolving and any satisfaction of its desire to confirm that what it takes to be true or right or good is; that this possible unity of itself with itself, as he said, "must become essential for it" and so that self-conscious consciousness should be understood as "desire." I took that claim to mean that the self-relation in question has got to involve the subject in some *attempt*, an attempt at what Hegel called a "unity" with itself because any such initial relation established is always provisional in the sense of revocable. (Consciousness is always "beyond itself" in his terms.) Some putative content might, for example, not be coherently integrable with another.

In Hegel's own terms, he also expressed this point by noting that self-consciousness was what he called a *movement* (*Bewegung*),[5] one that contained stages of development for both an individual's and a culture's "coming to self-consciousness" and that could be said to have an inherent teleological structure.

Now once we have introduced in this way the idea that self-consciousness is something to be achieved, we can introduce a discussion of the conditions of its successful (or "satisfying") realization, its self-certification in a way. And here Hegel's claim is just as bold and unusual as his original claim about desire: it is that self-consciousness "finds its satisfaction [the appropriate success-word if self-consciousness is desire] in another self-consciousness," or, going further, that a self-consciousness can actually *be* self-conscious *only* in "being recognized." This is the basis of what will be the most important result in this way of addressing the matter:

---

[5] "Es ist als Selbstbewußtsein Bewegung." PhG, ¶167. In ¶178, it is also called a *Prozess*.

that our answerability to the world is inextricably bound with, even dependent for its possibility on, our answerability to each other.[6]

III

This is not the way this section is usually interpreted. Let me briefly present the more conventional view of what Hegel is after in this depiction of a primal struggle to the death for recognition, leading to the establishment of unequal and oppressive social relations based on power and violence.

Hegel appears to be trying to make a contribution to a discussion that we recognize as a central one in all modern political and social thought. If we imagine the human condition prior to institutions and law, we might be able to imagine the nature of the resulting creation of institutional order and law and our stake in, and so the basic rationale for, such

[6] There are many differences between them, but a similar general idea is expressed by Donald Davidson in the course of his argument that one cannot be said to have a belief unless one can be said to have the concept of a belief; that this entails having the concept of an objective world (that what one believes might be false), and that *this* latter requires language, understood in its social, communicative dimension. That is:

> Our sense of objectivity is the consequence of another sort of triangulation, one that requires two creatures. Each interacts with an object, but what gives each the concept of the way things are objectively is the base line formed between creatures by language. The fact that they share a concept of truth alone makes sense of the claim that they have beliefs, that they are able to assign objects a place in the public world.
>
> The conclusion of these considerations is that rationality is a social trait. Only communicators have it.

Donald Davidson, "Rational Animals," in *Subjective, Intersubjective, Objective* (Oxford: Oxford University Press, 2001), p. 105.

norms. We can see why such institutions are unavoidable and would have to be willed by any rational agent.

So we imagine a kind of mythic picture of a form of life without established social bonds, and we get Rousseau's non-social solitary savage, Hobbes's terrified egoist, Locke's prudent, laboring individual, Rawls's "veiled contractor," and here with Hegel we imagine a putative situation without any normative constraints on action. Hegel then seems to be suggesting that the primordial human problem is one that can be described in these five steps.

1. The original situation is a simple problem of independence and dependence. One is either able to execute one's will, despite the opposition of others, or one's will is controlled, blocked, or otherwise determined by an other. There is no middle ground, no reason, on the radical hypothesis being entertained, to believe that anything can be assumed (any common value or basis for trust) to moderate or resolve this problem. (We need not decide whether such independence is of value for itself or just as a means to security, stability, and the preservation of life.) So Hegel's initial orientation is closest to Hobbes's picture, but he denies that there is any reason to think that everyone will see the advantages of a Leviathan state, rather than continued struggle. He argues that the willingness of any one party to insist on independence not as part of a strategy, but just in itself, *even at the risk or cost of life*, renders question-begging Hobbes's solution. (Hobbes recognizes this possibility of course—he worries about the persistence of vainglory—but comes close to writing it off as insane. For Hegel this assumption simply builds into the Hobbesean picture of reason what Hobbes wants to get out of it.)

2. This is therefore a situation of unavoidable conflict, *Kampf*, struggle. (It is, that is, on the simple assumption of finitude; that one's deeds will eventually conflict with or

impede what another would otherwise have been able to do. And by hypothesis, we have no grounds for assuming any appeal to common interests or mutual advantage. The initial condition is imagined as too treacherous and unstable.)

3. The struggle that ensues can end either with the death of both or the death of one. If the latter, the situation of uncertainty and challenge is not resolved, just postponed until another opponent shows up.

4. We have to be able to imagine a situation in which one refuses to submit, risks life, and the other submits, and this as something like the ground situation of all human social existence. The one who submits is not merely conquered, physically suppressed, but restrains *himself* in acknowledgment of the Master. (Like Freud, in Hegel drives of various sorts can be said to become human desire only when repressed, and in Hegel this will mean repressed in the face of a challenge by another.) And again, this is all under the assumption that the original human problem, the one that civilized order is a response to, is one of mastery and submission and who will occupy what position.

5. But the problem of the Master's independence is not resolved if this situation is something like a truce. The Bondsman must truly submit and acknowledge the Master's entitlement. But this acknowledgment is worthless to the Master because he is recognized by one whom he does not recognize and because the acknowledgment is coerced, cannot be assumed to be genuine submission, and so is dangerously more like a temporary truce than a victory. The Bondsman, by submitting, has for the Master been reduced to the level of animal life and so the Master's resolve to realize the mastery that he claims is thwarted. The Bondsman, by contrast, does not negate his attachment to life in the abstract, aristocratic way of the Master. Instead, he begins the long, slow process of liberating himself gradually from

nature, through labor, science, technology and so forth and eventually the utter dependence (and uselessness) of the Master are obvious for all to see and human beings can begin to entertain the hope of a genuine mutuality of recognition, equality before the law, liberal democratic institutions, equal rights protection and so forth.

There is a great deal about this account that is true and we shall return to elements of it. It involves the rather extraordinary claim that the unjustified exercise of mere power itself creates a form of dissatisfaction and suffering visited on those *exercising* such power, and in a way that makes it plausible to assume that such positions of domination and submission cannot long stand. But it is implausible that at this stage of the *Phenomenology*, Hegel would simply begin suddenly talking about social struggle and the achievement of mutuality of recognition like this, as if beginning the book again on a new topic. Our task, the task of any dedicated reader, is still to see how the rudiments of this account of the nature of our answerability to each other are relevant to, inextricable from, our answerability to the world, or our answerability to reason, as one could put it, and that requires an approach that continues the interpretation that extends from the Kantian framework noted above.

IV

The idea is that all determinate consciousness is, let us say, positional,[7] is something like *having a position* on what is

---

[7] Terry Pinkard, in *Hegel's Phenomenology: The Sociality of Reason* (Cambridge: Cambridge University Press, 1994), calls this "assuming a position in 'social space'" (p. 47) and goes on to say that "a 'move' in 'social space' is an inference licensed by that space" (ibid.). I think this is right,

its intentional object, or on what it is doing. It is to be understood as a taking, and it can only *be* positional, have a position, if this involves *taking a position* actively, or apperceptively. But this latter self-knowledge as an activity is *not* positional. It is not because its apperceptive self-awareness is not of an object but rather is something like the avowing of a practical commitment of a sort, something like a projecting (if we stay with the project language) of oneself outward into the world and the future; all in the same sense that knowing what I am doing is not observational or introspective. If I have such knowledge, it is *to be knowingly carrying on* in the appropriate way. (So what it is for me to be aware of my giving a lecture as I am giving it *is* for me to be continuously, now and into the future, actively if quite implicitly subscribing to, sustaining a commitment to, the norms of appropriateness for such an activity, something that certainly doesn't happen automatically, and can be disputed by others.[8] This stretching along or projecting or commitment-sustaining from the present into all appropriate contexts and futures is what I argued Hegel calls "desire" in its distinctly human form, and its satisfaction.[9]) As we saw,

---

and Pinkard's account in his Section One of Chapter Three ("Self-Consciousness and the Desire for Recognition") gives a clear but somewhat high-altitude picture of the course of the opening of Chapter Four. I am trying here to slow down a bit and to understand the details of the text. The account I am presenting is also different from the one I provided in "'You Can't Get There From Here': Transition Problems in Hegel's *Phenomenology of Spirit*," in *The Cambridge Companion to Hegel*, ed. F. Beiser (Cambridge: Cambridge University Press, 1993).

[8] Cf. Sebastian Rödl, *Self-Consciousness*, pp. ix, 9, and especially Chapter Two and Chapter Six.

[9] Even in activities like imagining, I am observing the normative requirements of imagining. I do not, as a consequence of the pleasure of imagining myself on the Costa Brava, leap into Lake Michigan. (*In* imagining I know that I am imagining without observing myself imagining.) It

Hegel's language for this is that the unity of consciousness "must become essential" for the subject, and he tells us that *this* means that "self-consciousness is desire itself." To some degree this means that no self-conscious consciousness can take up one "position" and no other. What it is to have one position is to be committed to the various inferences and exclusions and further commitments in the future in other situations that position or commitment would entail, many obviously not evident at the time of assertion, but which introduce the problem of self-unity and so the desiring dimension of carrying on in a way that realizes the commitments I have undertaken.

Now having a desire, even at the level of animal life, and responding to it in a way differentially geared to probable success, and altering what one does in the light of merely minimal success or failure is certainly a *form* of an intentional relation to the world. One could say, the world is "for one" in a way, and this is because one takes the world to be in various ways. One discriminates between food and non-food, potential mate or not and so forth. But in this sort of a picture one is simply *subject to* one's desire and subject to the fixed requirements of one's species-life, subject to what Hegel starts referring to as life itself. A consideration of the animal's life as a whole, even its form of life, is necessary for any of its orectic states to make sense as the state it is, but it is not necessary *for the animal*. The animal's desires and their pursuit are not experienced "in the light of" such a

---

would be a bit misleading to put it this way, but one way of summing this up: to say that self-consciousness is desire is to say that one unavoidably wants to be whoever one takes oneself to be, one seeks satisfaction that what one claims is as one claims, and one strives actually to realize the intention one avows. None of these desiderata, Hegel eventually wants to show, can be realized alone.

whole and the place and relative importance of such pursuits within it.

It is another thing altogether to be considered the *subject of a life*, actually to lead a life. Such a status would involve such a life being for the subject in some way, and would thus mean being the subject of commitments of one sort or another, to *take* the world to be in a way that counts as a claim and that comes with the assumptions of entitlement and the prohibitions of inconsistency (within such a whole). The Hegelian claim at issue now is that *what one needs to add* to the picture of a "differentially responsive desiring being with a mere sentiment of itself, of its life," in order to differentiate such mere systematic responsiveness from action on the basis of claims, commitments, entitlements, justifications, warrants, *is the presence of another subject* capable of challenging such a potential claimant. Only in the presence of such a challenge, goes the argument, does the subject's self-relation become normative, not a natural expression of animal desire. Why would he formulate the issue this way?

Before proceeding, though, a qualification is needed on the notion of "adding" something like this. I mean: what has to be in our picture of such an orectic being for it to be a recognizably human desirer? The idea is not that we and animals share a "level" of sentient responsiveness, and then we have another mental capacity somehow "added on" to such a shared sentient responsiveness. That would encourage a picture of self-consciousness as a self-monitoring of such sentient states, and that, as we have seen, would not be a picture of self-consciousness but simply of another level of consciousness. Our sentient responsiveness is *itself* self-conscious; the latter is not added on. Or, said another way, animals do not "lack" self-consciousness; are not "like us," but without self-consciousness. They "lack" self-consciousness only in the trivial and uninformative and potentially endless sense in which I "lack" invisibility, or omnipotence. They have animal sentience; we have another form because self-conscious, but we can add what is different, other, about such *self-conscious sentience* and that is the question pursued here; not an add-on question.

The answer can be formulated in the neo-pragmatic language made well known recently by Robert Brandom, and I want to take up a bit of his interpretation of this chapter as a way of exploring what Hegel might mean. The first Hegelian point that Brandom captures extremely well in his own terminology is that self-consciousness has a distinct characteristic: how I take myself to be is *self-constituting*; I *am* who I take myself to be or can only be said to be an I or subject insofar as I determinately take myself to be such and such, in some determinate way or other, and I accordingly functionally vary as such self-constituted takings vary. (In his *Philosophy of Subjective Spirit* in the *Encyclopedia*, Hegel writes: "spirit is essentially only what it knows of itself.")[10] Since such a self-relation is realized in deeds, fulfillments of projected commitments, I can also turn out not to be whom I took myself to be (or can turn out not to know what I took myself to know) but that erroneous self-conception is still an essential dimension of who I am. (I might *be* a fraud, for example, or self-deceived, and therein lies something crucial to my "self.")[11] So, as Brandom puts it, summing up one of the most momentous and influential claims of the *Phenomenology*, self-conscious beings do not have natures, they have histories. Human beings have taken themselves to be Christians, athletes, opera singers, spies, kings, professors, knights,

[10] PSS, vol. I, pp. 68–69.
[11] SDR, p. 128.

and so on. They only are such if they take themselves to be, and their taking themselves to be at least partially constitutes their being such.[12] And that is indeed Hegel's deepest point here and is stressed throughout many formulations. "Geist," he says, "is a product of itself," historically self-made over time.[13]

What I want to say is that Brandom, because he favors his own account (not Hegel's) of the relation between a causal perceptual interchange with the world and the role of sociality in the constitution of veridical claims (his "reliable differential responsive disposition" (RDRD), score-keeping account),[14] reintroduces the "two-step" account of the intuition-understanding relation, a story that Kant and Hegel were trying to avoid, and so Brandom isolates the issue of the social nature of self-consciousness in a way that is the mirror opposite of McDowell's account. Where McDowell's interpretation made Chapter Four look like a reconsideration, even if also a deepening and so an extension, of the issue of consciousness and object, of apperceptive intelligence and sensible receptivity, Brandom's is a "new topic" interpretation of Chapter Four. While McDowell is certainly not trying to deny that sociality and social dependence *will* play crucial roles in Hegel's account later, he denies that such themes are relevant *here*, and so tries to

---

[12] Only partially, because, as Brandom points out, one can fail to act in a way consistent with such a self-ascription, and so discover that one was not who one took oneself to be.

[13] PSS, I, pp. 6–7. I develop an extended interpretation of this claim in *Hegel's Practical Philosophy*.

[14] I won't try to give an account here of this theory. See, *inter alia*, Brandom's "The Centrality of Sellars' Two-Ply Account of Observation," in *Tales of the Mighty Dead* (Cambridge, Mass.: Harvard University Press, 2002), and pp. 388–90 of my "Brandom's Hegel," *European Journal of Philosophy* 13:3 (2005), pp. 381–408.

preserve a commonsense picture in which successful perception does not involve such social dependence,[15] Brandom
too distinctly isolates the sociality of self-consciousness.[16] I
think that McDowell's isolation of the sociality theme occurs
because he is generally suspicious of attributing any strong
role (or at least what *I* would call a strong or robust role)
to sociality in the conditions of perceptual knowledge itself.
That all seems to him implausibly complicating and coun-
ter to a more commonsense position. And McDowell's position is overall more Kantian and concentrates only on the
Hegelian account of the way conceptual activity shapes perceptual knowledge and intentional action. Brandom, on the
other hand, concentrates on the issue of self-consciousness
and sociality because he has his own quasi-Sellarsean theory
of perceptual content and the mind-world relation. What
I am trying to argue is that neither gets right the relation
between Chapter Four and the first three chapters.

The basic question at issue here is how to explain the necessary conditions for this self-constituting, and the terms of
Hegel's answer are well laid out by Brandom: what would we
have to *add* to the picture of an object's differential responsiveness to its environment (something that iron can do in
responding to humid environments by rusting and to other
environments by not rusting), from differential responses
that are intentional, that are not simply caused responses to

---

[15] Or at least, ultimately, any social dependence more complicated than
socialization into a linguistic community.

[16] Cf. for example his gloss on "Self-Consciousness is Desire itself." He
signals that he wants the discussion to be about the relation between self-
consciousness and erotic awareness as such, ". . . at least in the sense that
the most primitive form of self-awareness is to be understood as a development of the basic structure of erotic awareness" (SDR, p. 139).

the world, but which can be said to involve taking the world to be a certain way. This is the proto-intentionality typical of animals who, when hungry (and so desirous), can practically classify, take the objects in their environment *as* food (desire-satisfying). But differentially responding to food and distinguishing it from non-food does not satisfy hunger just ipso facto, as would be the case if we were still at the level of the iron responsiveness. (Responding in that case *is* rusting.) The animal must *do* something to satisfy its hunger and must do what is appropriate, sometimes involving several steps and even cooperation with other animals. It must get and eat such food. Another way of saying that the animal does not just respond to food items in its environment but takes things to be food is that there is now possible for the animal an appearance-reality distinction. It can take things to be food that are not and can learn from its mistakes. Or it only responds and acts to eat such food *when* it is hungry, when in a proto-intentional way, it takes the food as to-be-eaten *now*.[17]

And thus far, I think this tracks very well what Hegel is up to. Having conceded that without sensory interchange with the world, there is no possible knowledge about the world, he goes on to argue that such a perceptual interchange alone, or the mere matter of fact modification of our sensibility, cannot amount to a world we could experience. We must understand how things are taken to be what they are by subjects, and that means understanding the kind of beings for whom things can appear, and so be taken (apperceptively) to be such and such, or not; indeed, take things to

---

[17] "A desire is more than a disposition to act in certain ways, since the activities one is disposed to respond to objects with may or may not satisfy the desire, depending on the character of these objects" (SDR, p. 133).

be such and such in the light of their possibly not being so; a normatively attentive being. And this means understanding the difference between mere differential responsiveness, and a desiring, discriminatory consciousness, a practical classification (or "taking"), which is the most basic, minimal way of understanding how things can be for a subject, and not just serve as response-triggers. Noting this distinct capacity has gotten us to animal consciousness as proto-intentional.

The next step is the crucial one. *Now* what do we have to add to this picture to get not proto-intentionality but real intentionality; that is, not just something like a sentiment of one's life in play as one seeks to satisfy desire actively, differentially, and in practically successful ways, but genuine self-consciousness and practical self-determination (acting on reasons one can produce)?[18] What is it for a *self* to be *for itself* in all its engagements with the world and others, if it is not an introspectable object? One way to look at this, in line with what has been said, both in this section and before, is: we need to know what is necessary in order to introduce a distinction between what I take myself to be and what I am (or what I take myself to know and what I do know, or what I take myself to be doing and what I am doing), and we must do this without suggesting that one misapprehends oneself as an object (as if mistaking a dog for a wolf) or as if any direct confirmation of what one takes to be so is possible.[19]

---

[18] I mean "add" here in a purely figurative sense. It is not as if we have something that could be considered animal desire, and then some additional capacity besides. Once we have "built" a full picture of human orectic intentionality, the whole picture of our sentient lives, from "top to bottom," looks different.

[19] That would be like taking something to be Y on the basis of what one took to be X, and that would hardly help matters.

Rather, what is involved in so taking oneself is to attribute a certain determinate authoritative status to oneself, one that has to be provisional and subject to challenge.[20] That is, one can take hunger or the desire for food to be much more than an occasion or a stimulus to act, but to be a reason to act, *or not*. And "assuming command," as it were, of such determinations is to take oneself to be, authoritatively, *such a determiner*, "the decider," in the immortal words of our former president.

The question is: under what conditions would this *be* what it is *taken to be* (would so ascribing such authority to oneself be having such authority)? That is, it is always theoretically possible to see any such resolution or self-ascription or self-assertion to be the expression of some *other* desire, perhaps a complex psychological animal desire for dominance or self-sufficiency or whatever. In such a case one would still be just subject *to* one's desires, and actions would just *express* such orectic attitudes, whereas what we want is a subject *of* desire, a subject determining which desire is to be pursued and why, for reasons. It is in answer to this question that Hegel introduces as a necessary element in, as I am putting it, this "being what it is taken to be," and it is another self-ascribing subject whose position clashes with, renders impossible what would have been possible but for the presence of two such subjects and merely finite resources. This forces on a subject a question of commitment.[21] In a commitment, one is forced

[20] This is what we discussed earlier here in the phenomenological (in the Husserlian sense) language of "positional" consciousness.

[21] Honneth, "Von der Begierde zur Anerkennung: Hegels Begründung von Selbstbewußtsein," pp. 195 ff., claims that most commentators on this chapter fail to explain the transition from what he calls the experiencing subject's "disappointment over the independence of the object" and an

to resolve incompatibilities and sacrifice something; one is not just expressing a desire. To take oneself to be committed is to ascribe to oneself an authority that unavoidably involves an attitude toward an other. The most obvious is that in taking myself to be an authoritative taker I also establish a status that I have to concede is open to the other, if the same reasons for the commitment apply, and that I cannot deny to the other. It is in the presence of this sort of challenge that the implicit authority and status self-ascribed must be realized or not, will turn out to be in deed an actual such status and not another expression of the subject's subjection to the imperatives of life, or not. And that realization must involve the possibility of just such a claim to authority by another. Likewise, put a different way, such avowals could be in some psychological sense "sincere" but turn out to be inconsistent with what someone attributing to himself such an authority would have to say and do.

"encounter with the other and to recognition." I am arguing that this is the wrong way to look at this transition, that the ceaselessness of mere desire (being subject to one's desires) is a "disappointment" only from the view of the observing, philosophical "we" that always parallels and comments on the experience of the experiencing subject. (This is so because such a point of view already "knows" what the results of the first three chapters require, and why the self-relation characteristic of a merely orectic consciousness will not supply sufficient "independence.") All Hegel needs on that level is the assumption of simple finitude and scarcity, and the extreme possibility of a contesting subject who *pushes* the conflict "to the death," beyond merely natural attachments. It seems to me that in his commentary, Honneth invents an internal problem—the experiencing subject's sense of its own, all-negating, all-consuming "almightiness"— that I do not see in the text. That would be an extremely odd and wholly unmotivated delusion of omnipotence if it were there. Since this is the basis of Honneth's extended comparison with Winnicott (p. 199), I claim that this kind of gloss is not relevant to the argument of Chapter Four.

In making this clear, Hegel introduces a dramatic illustration that has become very well known, a "struggle to the death" for recognition. This is the beginning of the suggestion we have touched on before—that Hegel considers the distinct normative status of human subjects (as persons, agents) not as a reflection of some substantive or metaphysical nature, but as a social achievement of a kind and so as bound up with an inevitable and distinct form of social conflict. Here he begins by trying to make clear in a very simple way what it is to have achieved a kind of independence from the species-specific requirements of "life," and he claims that such an achievement is only possible in relation to others and that it is just that—something we *achieve*. (Human beings, *Geist*, make themselves into beings who ultimately hold themselves and others to account. They do not just interact and clash as the result of the contingent expressions of desire.)

We intuitively resist this picture and think that such a norm-responsiveness must be explained by some metaphysical distinction between the *kind* of thing we are and the *kind* of things animals and inanimate beings are. But there is never any appeal to this sort of metaphysics in Hegel's account. Desire-triggered responses are experienced as commitments when in some context *I am compelled to decide* what is important, what is significant, what perhaps weighs against life itself. This is not the emergence of a metaphysical distinctiveness, but the start of a new game that, as far as we know, only human animals can play, a language game, or *Geist*-game of holding each other to account by appealing to and demanding practical reasons, justifications for what emerge as claims of authority. What we want to know now is how such a game can be effectively played, the answer to which cannot be provided by attention to the biological properties of the beings or their evolutionary history.

In Brandom's summation of the point we have reached, he says,

> . . . what is required to be able to take something to be a self is to be able to attribute attitudes that have distinctively *normative* significances: to move from a world of *desires* to a world of *commitments, authority* and *responsibility*.[22]

In the extreme conditions imagined by Hegel, attributing a normative significance to myself or acknowledging someone's entitlement to claim authority cannot be merely expressions of sentiment or preference if what is at stake and can be risked is *all* attachments to life, desire, and so forth.[23] (The radical Hegelian claim, which need not be an issue here, is that *all* having such authority amounts to is being acknowledged—under the right conditions and in the right way—to have such authority.)[24] And if that is so then the

---

[22] SDR, p. 135.

[23] In Brandom's formulation: "For one to have that significance *for* oneself—not just being in oneself something things can be something *for*, but being that *for* oneself as well—that significance must be something things can be or have *for* one" (SDR, p. 139).

[24] This issues in a familiar "recognitional paradox." This statement of the radical claim, it might easily be argued, is incoherent. It can't be that one has the authority by being recognized to have it, because the recognizer recognizes on the basis of some reason to grant that authority. *That* reason cannot be "you merit recognition because I recognize you" without obvious circularity. If there must be such an internal ground for meriting recognition, then clearly someone can have an authority that is not recognized. The problem is an old one. In a sense it goes back to Aristotle's claim that honor cannot be the highest human good because one is honored for something higher than being honored; one is honored for what one did to deserve honor. And it is also obviously related to the Euthyphro discussion of piety. (Is the holy loved by the gods because it is holy, or is it holy because it is loved by the gods?) In this regard, cf.

relevant satisfaction or resolution of such an insistence cannot be just the submission or retreat of some other. The resolution must be a kind of acknowledgment, a recognition of the authority claimed in such a struggle. That is all that in this game would make authority authority. And so the desire inherent in all consciousness (consciousness being "beyond itself," such that its unity with itself "must become essential for it"), it has turned out, must be, cannot but be, a *desire* for recognition by others.[25] Just as we saw in our discussion of Kant, one cannot be said to be a reason-responsive being without being a creature of desire, striving to close the gap between claim and justification, intention and successful realization, action and legitimation. Likewise in Hegel's transformation of that point, in ascribing a certain normative, authoritative status to oneself, one cannot be said to be indifferent not only to those who practically prevent the realization of such claims, but also to those who challenge and reject such status altogether, and who can claim a like and conflicting authority for themselves.

How this all works is then spelled out by Brandom in ways quite close to his own account of the role of the social

the useful discussion of "misrecognition" in Heikki Ikäheimo and Arto Leitinen, "Analyzing Recognition," in *Recognition and Power*, ed. Bert van den Brink and David Owen (Cambridge: Cambridge University Press, 2007), pp. 53–56.

[25] Alexandre Kojève, who basically inflates this chapter to a freestanding, full-blown philosophical anthropology, made this point by claiming that for Hegel the distinctness of human desire is that it can take as its object something no other animal desire does: another's desire. This desire to be desired (to be properly recognized) amounts to the basic impulse or conatus of human history for Kojève. See *Introduction to the Reading of Hegel: Lectures on the* Phenomenology of Spirit, assembled by Raymond Queneau, ed. Allen Bloom, trans. James Nichols (Ithaca: Cornell University Press, 1969), pp. 3–30.

attribution of authoritative status as the required normativity essential to possible intentionality in general as well as essential to the possibility of self-consciousness:

> So specific recognition involves acknowledging another as having some authority concerning how things are (what things are Ks). When I do that, I treat you as one of us, in a primitive normative sense of 'us'—those of us subject to the same norms, the same authority—that is instituted by just such attitudes.[26]

However, there are various aspects of Brandom's account that do not match Hegel's in Chapter Four, and these divergences are related. His account is of course a reconstruction,[27] but for one thing, he leaves out an element that on the surface seems quite important to Hegel's sense of the case he is making. I mean his appeal to the experience of *opposed self-consciousnesses*. This concerns what Brandom has elsewhere called disparagingly the "martial" rhetoric of Chapter Four, especially the talk of a struggle to the death, which Brandom wants to treat as a metonymy, a figure of sorts for genuine commitment. (Regarded this way, being willing to risk anything important could show that the commitment functioned as a norm, not the expression of mere desire (or animal desire) alone.) But Hegel treats the extreme situation, the risk of life, as a key element *in* the story itself, not as an exemplification of a larger story (the making

---

[26] SDR, p. 142.

[27] In the language of *Tales of the Mighty Dead*, he is more interested in a *de re* interpretation than a *de dicto* one. That is, he wants to know not what the historical Hegel is committed to, but, given what that historical Hegel was committed to, what *would* he *have* to be committed to in another, perhaps more perspicuous, more contemporary vocabulary. See pp. 99–107. See also my "Brandom's Hegel."

explicit of the logical nature of commitment). It illustrates the possibility of an independence from all dependence on life itself.

I think that what Hegel tries to explain at this point is why it is that we cannot treat as satisfactory any picture of a monadically conceived self-conscious desiring consciousness, a desiring being who can practically classify and who is aware of being a practical classifier and so has a normative sense of properly and improperly classifying, but is imagined in no relation to another such self-conscious classifier or imagined to be indifferent to another's construals and claims, his takings. This is inadequate on the simple empirical premise that there are other such subjects around in a finite world, which subjects *will not and from their point of view cannot allow* such pure self-relatedness. Brandom is right that what distinguishes holding a commitment from merely expressing a desire is a willingness to alter or give up the commitment if it conflicts with others. One wouldn't be committed to anything if one knowingly accepted inconsistent commitments. And Hegel asks us to imagine how an inescapable conflict with others attempting to satisfy their desires forces on one the *nature* of one's attachment to life. It is in response to such conflict that the relation can now count as a commitment, given that one surrendered or sacrificed the original commitment for the sake of life. *Life has become a value*, not a species imperative. But the sketch we have so far of a self-conscious theoretical and practical intentionality insures not only that there will be this contention, but that on the premises we have to work with so far, *it has to be* a profound contention that can, initially or minimally conceived, only be resolved by the death of one, or the complete subjection of one to the other. This will play a large role in Hegel's account of the sociality on which we are said by him to depend.

V

Here are some examples of passages where Hegel makes such claims. The important remarks occur after ¶175. There Hegel contrasts the satisfaction of animal desire, whose subject, following Brandom, takes things a certain way, differentially discriminates, but then simply negates these objects, or satisfies its desire. Such a subject may be resisted in a sense by one's desired object fighting back, if we are talking about predator and prey. But such resistance is just not a challenge, more like an obstacle. (No challenge to the correctness of the classifications or the entitlement to make them has been made.) With this sort of negation of one's object, another desire arises. That is:

> Desire and the certainty of itself achieved in its satisfaction are conditioned by the object, for the certainty exists by way of the act of sublating of this other. For this act of sublating even to be, there must be this other. (¶175)

In this situation, to revert to the language we have used several times, one cannot be said to be the subject of one's desires but subject to one's desires. One's putative independence as the subject of one's thoughts and deeds is actually a form of dependence, and so one's takings cannot yet be counted as normative takings.

That is, one is subject to the endless cycle of desire and satisfaction and cannot be said to have achieved any "distance" from one's desires, any independent point of view on them:

> Self-consciousness is thus unable by way of its negative relation to the object to sublate it, and for that reason it

once again to an even greater degree re-engenders the object as well as the desire.

This all changes however, when, among the objects of self-consciousness's orectic attitudes there is an object which is not an object but another potential subject, which, *as such a subject*, cannot simply be "negated" (only destroyed as an object), but if it is to satisfy the desire of the first subject, "must in itself effect this negation of itself." (He puts it less abstractly in ¶182: "For that reason, it can do nothing on its own about that object if that object does not do in itself what the first self-consciousness does in it.") Another subject (challenging rather than impeding my satisfaction of desire, and this by forcing the issue "to the death") is inaccessible to me as such a subject, unreachable by direct force or coercion. Whatever relation is to be established must be effected *by* that subject; he must "do in itself what the first self-consciousness does in it."

VI

At this point we must remember all the way back to our discussion of ¶80 in the first chapter, and state these results in terms of the original problem. That passage included the claim that a self-conscious consciousness is always "beyond itself" and that the problem this engenders, the unity of self-consciousness with itself, "must become essential" to self-consciousness. One form of such satisfaction is simple desire satisfaction; unity with self is produced by eliminating the gap or need within the self, the desire. This is though only a temporary satisfaction; there are always new and manifold desires stimulated, to which one is subject.

But another sort of satisfaction altogether is at issue when one's claims or takings as such are confronted by another who denies them, who has his own claims, or when one's deeds, inevitably affecting what others would otherwise be able to do, are rejected, not merely obstructed, by a being whose deeds conflict with one's own.[28] The achievement of such a unity is not then possible alone. As Hegel will go on to show, one will not have responded to such challenges as the challenges they are (a resolution of unity of such disparity will not have become "essential to it") by simply annihilating the other, and so one will not have satisfied oneself, or achieved the unity (self-satisfaction) spoken of so frequently. (One would still be in the position of an animal desirer, endlessly subject to one's desires.) The presence of another "taker who takes himself to be a taker" and so who is a potential challenge, not just an obstacle, establishes that the normative problem, whether one's takes on the world are as they ought to be, or are worth what one had assumed, is "essential" to this self-reconciliation. That means that this confrontation of affirmation and negation cannot be resolved on, let us say, the animal level. That is, "*Self-consciousness attains its satisfaction only in another self-consciousness.*" Or, "Only thereby does self-consciousness in fact exist, for it is only therein that the unity of itself in its otherness comes to be for it" (¶177).

---

[28] Brandom's account and his account of Hegel tend to leap over this stage in the assemblage of what is necessary for a satisfying sociality: who gets to decide, and how, whether any authority claimed is one actually entitled. I have argued elsewhere that his talk of social negotiation over such issues is (as Brandom himself suspects) too irenic; assumes too much that Hegel wants to put in play as dialectically complex and problematic and ultimately as initiating a complex historical turn in philosophy altogether. See the discussion in my "Brandom's Hegel."

But in Hegel's account, there is no non-question-begging criterion, or method, or procedure or standard by which such a contention can be resolved. Whatever one might count as the giving and asking for reasons might be counted by the other as the arbitrary expression of the other's desire for success, as a mere instrumental ploy or strategy.[29] So, Hegel reasons, the primitive expression of normative commitment, the only available realization (*Verwirklichung*) of the claim *as a claim*, is a risk of life itself:

> [T]he *exhibition* of itself as the pure abstraction of self-consciousness consists in showing itself to be the pure negation of its objective mode, that is, in showing that it is fettered to no determinate *existence*, that it is not at all bound to the universal individuality of existence, that it is not shackled to life. (¶187)

Hegel makes such a claim not because of any anthropological position about the centrality of honor in human life. He claims what he does because he is trying to assemble the central, minimal elements of genuinely human sociality among self-conscious beings, a sociality that can provide the satisfaction he has argued arises as a problem with the realization that consciousness is always "beyond itself." And he is insisting that in this assembling, we must begin without begging any questions. So he proposes we think of the

---

[29] Here the reappearance in modern philosophy of a problem as old as the Sophists: the difficulty of distinguishing between putative appeals to reason and rhetorical strategies for maintaining positions of power, a problem that would intensify in Nietzsche and reach its culmination of sorts in Foucault. Hegel of course argues that this distinction *can* be made, but not by an appeal to an eternal/substantive standard or to any formal criteria.

problem as a struggle within such narrow parameters, and
we get this famous picture of everything being at stake:

> The relation of both self-consciousnesses is thus deter-
> mined in such a way that it is through a life and death
> struggle that each *proves his worth* to himself, and that both
> *prove their worth* to each other. (. . . daß sie sich selbst und
> einander durch den Kampf auf Leben und Tod *bewähren*.)
> (¶187)[30]

Throughout the rest of the chapter, Hegel shows the
practical incoherence of any attempted resolution of such
conflict by the establishment of mere power, or coerced
recognition. It is clear that what is ultimately necessary for
such a conciliation, for beings conceived as Hegel now has,
is some resort to practical reason and so ultimately some
shared view of a universal reconciliation.[31] And Hegel has a
"pragmatic" or a "historicized" or "dialogical"[32] view of what
counts as the appeal to reasons that is consistent with this
whole picture. He understands practical reason as a kind of
interchange of attempts at justification among persons, each
of whose actions affects what others would otherwise be able
to do, and all this for a community at a time. (What counts

[30] This language of "proof," "tests," and so forth is absolutely central to
what Hegel means by the "realization" of a concept or norm, and plays
the central role in what Hegel means by the opposition between subjective certainty and truth throughout the book, and in his important argument in Chapter Five where he denies the "inner intention causing
external bodily movements" picture of action in favor of what he calls
an "inner-outer speculative identity." For a more detailed account of this
view, see my *Hegel's Practical Philosophy: Rational Agency as Ethical Life*.

[31] Cf. Pinkard's concise summary of the problem, *Hegel's Phenomenology*,
p. 57.

[32] I mean the link between dialogic activity and rationality assigned to
Plato in Gadamer's book *Plato's Dialogical Ethics*, trans. Robert Wallace
(New Haven: Yale University Press, 1991).

as instances of such attempts, that is, changes over time.) But his account of what these attempts at mutual justification consist in requires in effect the rest of the book, the developmental and experiential procedure characteristic of a "phenomenology."

VII

"Self-Consciousness is desire itself." I have argued that Hegel means by this, once he has distinguished mere desire from human desire, that the apperceptive element in all thought and action is not self-regarding but "self-positing," or something like, in both McDowell's and Brandom's terms, taking responsibility, claiming authority for, what one thinks and does. In Hegel's account it is possible to imagine a transition of sorts between a primitive, still naturally explicable version of such a taking to a full-fledged, self-conscious, authority-claiming status only in the presence and especially challenge of another such self-conscious being. This is the beginning of a socially mediated conception of intentionality as such. But at this early stage in his account, we are not entitled to assume any prior agreement about the rules of reason in resolving the struggle for recognition, rules for the acknowledgment of the genuine authority of one's claims that must inevitably arise as problematic under the premises of Hegel's account thus far. Accordingly, within the assumptions Hegel allows himself, such a confrontation can only be resolved in the crudest of terms, by a fight to the death. This establishes whose claims are in fact claims *made by a subject* rather than the expression of life's imperatives because the struggle pushes the issue to the point where a complete indifference to life's imperatives determines the result. For each subject, this putative confrontation raises the question of whether one's existence as a living natural being is paramount, or whether one will ascribe to oneself the authority to determine the fate of one's existence as a subject of, not subject to, one's life. This relation to natural life and so the distinct status of a human subject is, as we have been saying throughout, something that must be achieved. The self-relation in relation to objects and others must be achieved, is a practical phenomenon inseparable from a relation with and initially an unavoidable struggle with, others. Genuinely human mindedness, the soul, spirit, the variety of designations for the distinctly human, are all going to be read through the prism of this idea that such a distinction is fundamentally a result, what will eventually emerge as a historical achievement.

Now Hegel is not of course suggesting that the resultant social statuses of Lord (*Herr*) and Bondsman (*Knecht*) represent a stable social achievement or resolution of the problem posed; just the opposite. He sets out immediately revealing its instability and unsatisfactory and so temporary status. Famously, the Lord must remain unsatisfied because he is recognized by one whom he does not recognize as capable of acknowledging authority. He sees the bondsman as little more than an animal, attached to animal life. The Lord does not appreciate, as the slave ultimately will, that the bondsman has in effect chosen life as a *value*, a choice that constitutes (ultimately), we might say, the modern or bourgeois form of life. And the Bondsman recognizes someone who does not recognize him, so has not yet achieved the initial status of authoritative recognizer. But, Hegel explains, the Bondsman is now in a position to understand that the stark opposition between attachment to or independence from life is a false opposition and can begin the slow work or "labor of the Concept" in freeing himself from his natural dependence and thereby eventually from the Master, who grows increasingly dependent on the Bondsman. In this context, one can understand how and why Hegel thinks of human freedom as a historical and social achievement, not a metaphysical or any other sort of property of the human as such. And all of us are well aware of the extraordinarily powerful impact such a notion would have outside of philosophy in the nineteenth and twentieth centuries.

Concluding Remarks

IN ¶184, HEGEL SUMS UP what he takes himself to have shown to be the basic "movement," as he calls it, of self-consciousness. Self-consciousness, that is, is never the direct presence of anything like a "self-object" to itself; it is a processual or dynamic self-relation that is to be achieved. Self-constituting self-construals (taking oneself to know something or taking oneself to be committed to doing something) are as mere avowals only provisional and are redeemable as such only in the future and with others. We have just seen why Hegel thinks that such a self-consciousness, construed this way, can only find its "satisfaction," can only redeem those "self-certainties" in "truth," *in "another self-consciousness."* He now says that such a movement, so construed, must be about an attempt at *recognition*; to any putative pair of opposed self-consciousnesses must be ascribed an inherent practical teleology, the ultimate outcome of which is that "They recognize themselves as mutually recognizing each other" (¶184).

By inherent teleology he means to say that the attempted fulfillment of a desire (and the self-relation characteristic of desire) can be imagined to be experienced differently in a situation of conflict, especially ultimate conflict. One can be imagined to have to determine what is worth fighting for, why, what value life has and so forth. (In this sense a *practical* teleology just means a discovered expansion of the "in order to" structure characteristic of action. One can be presumed to discover, in trying to satisfy one's desire under certain limited assumptions, that the assumptions must be changed and the formulation of the practical project itself must be reconceived.) But this alteration also means that one's avowals of commitments, importance, significance, what is essential to oneself and so forth, now understood as claims against another, contending self-consciousness, are thereby also understood as expressed with some claim to authority. And as we have seen, they can only be asserted if they are asserted with some assumption of normative force; otherwise they would just be expressions of reactions to various internal pushes and pulls of desires, passions, fears and so forth. I could not be said to be avowing a commitment if I am indifferent to denials of its realization, or indifferent to inconsistencies with other claims I avow. (It is in this sense that consciousness itself is for Hegel essentially a rational phenomenon.) In the presence of an imagined extreme challenge by another "taker," the projected satisfaction of a desire now must count as a *claim* against the other's attempt. If that is so, then the assertion of such a claim is also the attribution to oneself of an authority to make it. But such a self-attribution would not be the attribution of authority unless one understood the difference between merely attributing the authority to oneself and actually *having* such authority. At the stage of mere conflicting claims of authority, Hegel suggests that only one sort of step, consistent with the limited premises of such an account, will settle such an issue: the submission by one party to another, acknowledging such an authority under such a threat; one that can only be understood at this point as motivated by (practically rationally justified by) an unwillingness to risk everything on the authority claim, an unwillingness to die.

This assumption of a "fight to the death," a raising of the stakes beyond what any attachment to life could explain, is meant then to short-circuit any interpretation that remains at the animal or natural, or desire-triggered level. And so, just in themselves, such avowals raise the question of their own success-conditions, the relation between subjective self-certainty, and truth, in Hegel's frequent formulations. I can avow all sorts of entitlements to things, demand to be treated in a certain way, insist that the status I assert for myself should *be* the status I have in the world, and so forth. But avowing it doesn't make it so, and I cannot be indifferent to the relevant realization of what is demanded or claimed. (And there is no indication that Hegel has lost sight here of the breadth of this issue. The authority of epistemic claims and commitments is also part of this story.)

This inherent condition (for putative claims to authority really *being* authoritative) is something Hegel now begins to treat as a matter of social acknowledgment. What it is for such a claim to authority or normative force or entitlement to have authority or so forth, is for it to be acknowledged as such by others. But as the quotation above indicates, this is not something resolved by mere matter of fact acceptance. (Most of the subsequent narrative in the PhG is all about failed attempts at the establishment of the right recognitive relation, after the establishment of what had been taken to be satisfactory.) That recognitive relation must satisfy certain conditions if the recognition is to do what the claimant to normative force requires. (We learn *what* conditions by seeing what their absences mean for the experiencing consciousness.) It must be mutual; or to say it more strongly and clearly, must satisfy the conditions of genuine mutuality. In the language Kojève uses, to assert and claim one's desire in the face of any such challenge, is already to desire "something non-natural"—it is to desire another's desire (a desire to be desired), the other's relating to oneself as one relates to, avows commitments in the name of, oneself. One cannot coerce this, merely trick the other into granting it, Jacob and Esau like, or be indifferent to the issue without losing one's own hold on the claim as a claim to authority, one with genuine normative force. So the only condition in which the authority of one's self-constituting self-construals can be "true" is the condition of genuine mutuality.[1]

This means that those normative considerations that emerge from the imagined *Kampf* must be in some clear sense genuinely accepted by the other, something only the

---

[1] Against this whole approach, John McDowell has urged, in "Toward a Reading of Hegel on Action in the 'Reason' Chapter of the *Phenomenology*," in HWV that in making something like agency or authority dependent on actually being acknowledged as such, bad philosophy is being unnecessarily foisted onto Hegel. "We can respect a constitutive connection between the status and a *possibility* of its being acknowledged, without needing to accept that it is *conferred* by acknowledgement—that one has it by being taken to have it" (169). But there are two senses of "possibility" here. One involves the claim that one need not be actually and literally acknowledged by some real others in some continuous stretch of time in order to count as having the status. "Possibly" being so acknowledged is all one needs, but one maintains the view that one has such a status or authority *thanks to the (possible) acknowledgment by others in one's community*. The other sense implies that one simply *has* the status or authority (full stop) and it could possibly be acknowledged by others (because one actually has it, in itself), but they would then just be noting an independent normative fact. The latter is not a Hegelian thought, and the former is all I (or Hegel) need. Moreover, McDowell does not note that such authority is not simply, or as a matter of mere fact, "conferred." As noted, most of what Hegel discusses are attempts to confer it that fail, and what is interesting about his account is how he works his way toward eventual success.

other can manage and which I cannot coerce; and vice-
versa with respect to the other's claims on me. They must
be claims and considerations that can be shared, and this
immediately sounds a final Kantian reverberation. For Kant
had also made his own (non-phenomenological) case for the
practical inescapability of the claims of reason in anything
we do. I cannot be said to be acting at all, to be an agent, ex-
cept insofar as I act on reasons, and Kant thought he could
show that such reasons cannot be egoistic, but must be of
the form that could be shared in order to count as reasons
at all (that is, for *me*). So, I would suggest, the difference
between Kant and Hegel does not concern this core issue,
which they agree on. Kant famously thought at this point
that such a sharability requirement (mutuality of recognitive status, in his language, universality) could be satisfied
just in consideration of the *form* of the reason, or policy
maxim I give myself. Adopt no maxim that could not at the
same time serve as a universal law for all. (Although he also
seemed to think an equivalent formulation was: always act
as a member of the Kingdom of Ends; act in such a way that
you consider not just yourself but everyone as an autonomous rational setter of ends and adopt no maxim inconsistent with the existence of such a Kingdom; a formulation
much closer to the Hegelian insistence on mutuality of recognitive status.)

Here Hegel veers sharply away from Kant on this issue
of resolving what *counts* as the realization of true mutuality,
universality, sharability of claims for normative authority.
For he begins his account by pointing to such an ultimate
ideal resolution, but by methodologically conceding, in effect, that we have no determinate idea ex ante (and can have
no immediate intuitions about) what such genuine mutuality

consists in. As in so many other accounts, he proposes a developmental, not an analytic or deductive approach, in this case from a minimally normative but internally unsatisfying claim to such a basis for recognition (the Master-Bondsman relation, which the Master and the Bondsman take to be more than matter of fact power, but a rights relation, as it should be "because of" the Master's victory) and then showing gradually the internal strains and incompatible commitments such a presumption gives rise to. Thus, perhaps with Kant's chief category in mind, he says:

> The individual who has not risked his life may admittedly be recognized as a *person*, but he has not achieved the truth of being recognized as a self-sufficient self-consciousness. (¶187)

Hegel is here conceding that we can already say we have come to understand the formal character of mutuality, but he is also insisting that without some experiential, development account, one that begins with the centrality of conflict, to the death, and the reactive attempts to make sense of the results, we will never be able to resolve what such genuine mutuality amounts to.

There are two important new developments in Chapter Four that follow from this setup. The first is Hegel's account of the significance or meaning of the Bondsman's work, when that work is considered as performed in abject servitude. The important point Hegel makes is that when viewed historically (and from quite a high altitude), the Bondsman's work is inevitably educative, transformative. Work is said to be "desire held in check" (*gehemmte Begierde*) (¶195) and thereby something that educates ("*bildet*"). The result is that the Bondsman gradually begins to acquire a "mind of his own" (. . . *dies Wiederfinden seiner durch sich selbst eigner Sinn*). And this occurs with, in effect, everything at stake—life and death—because the Bondsman always labors in submission to the true master and Master, the fear of death.

This existential fable is in effect Hegel's response to Rousseau's declensionist narrative in his second *Discourse*, where the division of labor, and the beginning of the ever more complex and intricate forms of human dependence that it brings with it, is regarded as the beginning of a kind of social slavery. In Hegel's account, this dependence, like the fear of the Master, is the beginning of wisdom, here a kind of practical wisdom as it is the Master who grows ever more dependent (to the point, finally, of utter uselessness),[2] and it is the Bondsman who starts to achieve the slow conquest of nature and so liberates himself from the natural attachments responsible for his servitude in the first place.[3]

Second, Hegel suggests a way of understanding a difficulty that must emerge from his own account so far. The self-attribution of authority is like the having of a propositional attitude, a belief, say. As we have been discussing throughout, post-Kant and after his apperception thesis, the assumption is that one can only actually have a belief if one has the concept of belief, as in: one can come to have the belief that

---

[2] In the PhG, especially, VI.B.I., "The world of selfalienated spirit."

[3] This is what it all means "for us." For consciousness, at such an initial stage, nothing is as clear as all this. Cf.

> Because not each and every one of the ways in which his natural consciousness was brought to fruition was shaken to the core, he is still attached *in himself* to determinate being. His having a mind of his own is then merely *stubbornness*, a freedom that remains bogged down within the bounds of servility. . . . the form is a skill which, while it has dominance over some things, has dominance over neither the universal power nor the entire objective essence. (¶196)

one's prior belief was wrong.[4] In this case, ascribing any authority to oneself requires some sense of what it is actually to have such authority, as opposed to merely affirming that one does. The normative relation between the Master and the Bondsman, however, involves an understanding of the basis of the authority exercised by the Master that each also knows to be profoundly flawed. The Bondsman submits to the Master for the sake of his life; the Master exercises his authority in the name of his indifference to mere life. But the slave's acknowledgment is worthless to the Master, and the Master withholds any real recognition of the Bondsman. Each in a general sense takes back with one hand what is proffered by another, and must find a way of understanding their untenable and unstable situation. They must, because just as you cannot avow a commitment that is knowingly inconsistent with another commitment, you cannot attribute an authority which you also undermine or know cannot be based on what you take it to be based on. If the Master has no real authority, there is no way truly to internalize and live out such a submission. And if the Bondsman is not a possibly recognizing other, then the Master's claim to authority is empty and unsecured.

Hegel's unusual suggestion at this point begins quite a different way of understanding what normally would be taken to be various possible philosophical and religious options. Hegel understands them, Stoicism, Skepticism, and the Unhappy Consciousness, as a way of, in effect, compensating for and evading the situation just described:

> Within thinking, I *am free* because I am not in an other; rather, I remain utterly in my own sphere, and the object, which to me is the essence, is in undivided unity my

---

[4] Cf. the discussion of Davidson in footnote 6 of Chapter One.

being-for-myself; and my moving about in concepts is a movement within myself. (¶197)

And:

Ever since it made its conscious appearance in the history of spirit, this freedom of self-consciousness has, as is well known, been called *stoicism*. Its principle is this: that Consciousness is the thinking essence and that something only has essentiality for consciousness, or is true and good for it, only insofar as consciousness conducts itself therein as a thinking creature. (¶198, translation modified)

What was noted earlier as Hegel's unusual approach to such a position ("I can be free even in chains as long as I remain a 'thinking essence,'" and so forth) is quite clear at the end of ¶199:

As a universal form of the world-spirit, it can *only come on the scene in a time of universal fear and servitude* which is, however, also a time of universal cultural maturation which has raised culturally educative activity all the way up to the heights of thought. (My emphasis)

This kind of approach—that we can only fully appreciate what is actually being claimed by Stoic philosophy, what the full content of the Stoic position consists in, by understanding it as a form of "world spirit" and as appropriate to "a time of universal fear and servitude"—is also applied to Skepticism and the version of Christianity to which Hegel gives the dramatic name, "The Unhappy Consciousness." In each case he also tries to develop internal deficiencies in the positions that are themselves reflections of the unsuccessful normative self-understandings of the relevant types. Stoicism results in a sweeping, abstract, and indeterminate (and so finally unsatisfying) appeal to mere "thinking" as such; Skepticism's universal and relentless negation of any claim and value finally becomes self-negating; the Unhappy Consciousness exists in a state of self-division and self-contradiction that cannot be coherently or practically maintained. In its growing self-awareness, such an Unhappy Consciousness ultimately will learn to seek its "unity with itself"—that elusive desideratum that has been with us since ¶80 of the Introduction—not in a "Beyond" but in all of reality as itself rational, by ultimately, as Reason, "being certain of being all reality" (¶230).[5]

But both this approach and the claims themselves are controversial enough for a lengthy separate discussion. Our interest throughout has been on Hegel's two extraordinary claims—that self-consciousness is desire, and that self-consciousness finds its satisfaction only in another self-consciousness—and I hope that what has been said has justified such extensive attention to these dramatic formulations.

---

[5] This also means that we are back at an issue that bothers McDowell, who rightly asks (especially in his *Owl of Minerva* response, forthcoming): if the antithesis so problematic in the Consciousness chapters had been between an independent, spontaneous intelligence, and a dependent, sensibility-bound receptivity, how is a discursus on inter-personal relations supposed to help resolve *that* antithesis? What I have tried to show is that Hegel demonstrates that the antithesis problem is revealed to be one about claim-making authority and the problematic status of any self-ascribed authority. This becomes the issue it is under challenge from another, and with the structure of that relation and struggle, and so the problem of universality, on the table, he can return to the question of such authority (in claims about the world) as (ultimately) a matter of the nature of our claims on one another.

Index